The Essential Guide to
Understanding Special Educational Needs

The Essential Guide to Understanding Special Educational Needs

Jenny Thompson

Longman
is an imprint of

PEARSON

Harlow, England • London • New York • Boston • San Francisco • Toronto • Sydney • Singapore • Hong Kong
Tokyo • Seoul • Taipei • New Delhi • Cape Town • Madrid • Mexico City • Amsterdam • Munich • Paris • Milan

PEARSON EDUCATION LIMITED

Edinburgh Gate
Harlow CM20 2JE
United Kingdom
Tel: +44(0)1279 623623
Fax: +44(0)1279 431059
Website: www.pearsoned.co.uk

First published in Great Britain in 2010

© Pearson Education Limited 2010

The right of Jenny Thompson to be identified as author of this work has been asserted
by her in accordance with the Copyright, Designs and Patents Act 1988.

Pearson Education is not responsible for the content of third party internet sites.

ISBN: 978-1-4082-2500-4

British Library Cataloguing-in-Publication Data
A CIP catalogue record for this book can be obtained from the British Library

Library of Congress Cataloging-in-Publication Data
Thompson, Jenny.
  The essential guide to understanding special educational needs / Jenny Thompson.
      p. cm.
    ISBN 978-1-4082-2500-4 (pbk.)
    1. Special education--Great Britain. 2. Children with disabilities--Education--Great
Britain. 3. Special education teachers--Great Britain--In-service training. I. Title.
    LC3986.G7T56 2010
    371.90941--dc22
                                    2010006216

10 9 8 7 6 5 4 3 2 1
14 13 12 11 10

Set by 3
Printed and bound in Great Britain by Ashford Colour Press Ltd, Gosport, Hants

Contents

About the author

Jenny Thompson is a Senior Lecturer at the University of Derby on the Education Studies programme. She is also the Disability Coordinator for the School of Education at the university. Jenny has in excess of ten years teaching experience in special education schools, further education colleges and latterly in higher education.

Publisher's acknowledgements

We are grateful to the following for permission to reproduce copyright material:

'Medical model of disability and segregation', 'Needs model of disability and integration' and 'Social model of disability and inclusion' in Chapter 1, Reproduced by permission of SAGE Publications, London, Los Angeles, New Delhi and Singapore, from Gibson, S. and Blandford, S., *Managing Special Educational Needs*, Copyright © Suanne Gibson and Sonia Blandford, 2005; Figure 1.2 from the Democracy Disability and Society Group (DDS Group), The Thistle Foundation; Figures 3.1 and 3.2 Reproduced by permission of SAGE Publications, London, Los Angeles, New Delhi and Singapore, from Hughes, L. and Cooper, P., *Understanding and Supporting Children with ADHD*, Copyright © Lesley Hughes and Paul Cooper 2007; Figure 4.2 from Hunter–Carsch, M., Tiknaz, Y., Cooper, P. and Sage, R (eds), *The Handbook of Social, Emotional and Behavioural Difficulties* , Continuum International Publishing Group, 2006, reproduced by kind permission of *Continuum International Publishing Group*; Table on page 73 reproduced with permission from page 13, *Dyspraxia; A Guide for Teachers and Parents*, Ripley, K., Daines, B. and Barrett, J., (1997) London: David Fulton; Table on page 88 Reproduced by permission of SAGE Publications, London, Los Angeles, New Delhi and Singapore, from Pittman, M., *Helping pupils with autistic spectrum disorders to learn*, Copyright © Mary Pittman, 2007; Extract in Chapter 8 with permission from RNID. RNID is the charity working to create a world where deafness or hearing loss do not limit or determine opportunity, and where people value their hearing. We work by campaigning and lobbying, raising awareness of deafness and hearing loss, promoting hearing health, providing services and through social, medical and technical research; Extracts in Chapter 9 reproduced with permission from *Teaching Children with Visual Impairment: A Guide to Making the School Curriculum Accessible*, Salisbury, R., (2008), Abingdon: Routledge.

Every effort has been made by the publisher to obtain permission from the appropriate source to reproduce material which appears in this book. In some instances we may have been unable to trace the owners of copyright material and would appreciate any information that would enable us to do so.

Author's acknowledgements

I owe much to the children and young people who have contributed to this book indirectly, and I am also grateful to the many colleagues with whom I have worked over the years who have shared their experiences with students as teachers, who have provided enrichment to this book. I extend my thanks to Melanie Coultas, who has inspired my writing on the role of the SENCO.

I give special thanks to Catherine Yates at Pearson Education for her support and guidance, and her many invaluable suggestions during my writing this book; and to Katy Robinson for her continued support throughout the writing process.

I extend particular thanks to my husband Max, and my daughter Katie, who have always encouraged me, and to my good friend Vanessa for her endless patience and support during all the stages of writing this book.

I would also like to thank Vivienne Walkup for her constant encouragement during the writing process.

Introduction

In light of the Warnock Report (1978), commissioned by the government, and the UK legislation introducing the term 'special educational needs' (SEN), inclusion is high on the agenda in the UK. The Special Educational Needs and Disability Act 2001 (SENDA), strengthens the right of children with SEN to attend a mainstream school. In January 2007 the Department of Children, Schools and Families (DCSF) reported 229,110 pupils with special educational needs in England, of which 57.1 per cent were receiving mainstream education (DCSF, 2007). The vision of inclusion is paramount; this is becoming a reality in schools and the strategy for SEN, 'Removing Barriers to achievement' (DfES, 2004), was introduced to enable the principles of the SEN legislation to be taken further (DCSF, 2007):

> *Pupils with SEN in mainstream schools are able to play a full part in school life and receive a curriculum and teaching relevant to their needs.*

Training for professionals in schools and those training to teach is inconsistent and in some cases non-existent. Training may be limited to as little as a few hours as part of the general professional studies and given the scope of SEN, it would be impossible for newly qualified teachers (NQTs) to feel confident in dealing with each disability. As a result of insufficient training, trainees are entering the classroom ill-equipped to cope with the everyday challenges and demands that working in an inclusive classroom poses. My own experience both from working in schools and from feedback received via trainees and NQTs demonstrates a lack of confidence and the basic skills needed to understand and support children with special educational needs.

This book is an attempt to provide a framework for trainees, NQTs and the wider school workforce working alongside individuals with SEN. The book aims to be a practical, student-friendly, 'hands-on' resource for use in the classroom. It considers children and young people with special educational needs and encourages us to explore our beliefs and practices relating to these young learners. By considering children with a variety of special educational needs we will be better equipped to meet the needs of all children and young people in our educational settings.

This book will show you that the earlier you identify a pupil with special educational needs the easier it is to cater for those individual needs and ensure an inclusive approach to education.

A key aim of the book is to show you how to identify different special educational needs and offer you guidance and advice on how to cater for those needs. If pupils' needs are catered for, and they are supported with their work in order to achieve, they will be much more motivated to learn and you will enjoy teaching them too.

This book is exactly what the title says: 'an essential guide to understanding special educational needs' and I hope you enjoy reading it. Good luck!

How can I use this book effectively?

The Essential Guide to Understanding Special Educational Needs was written so that the reader is able to dip in and out of it, rather than starting at Chapter 1 and working through the whole book. In order to get the most out of the book I recommend you start by reading the first two chapters as these offer an overview of the history of SEN and also demonstrate how SEN is identified in an educational environment.

The overview in Chapter 1 includes various Acts of Parliament that have had an influence on the education of pupils with SEN. It also offers contrasting ideas concerning the medical model of disability and the social model of disability, and their impact on the inclusion of SEN pupils in mainstream educational environments.

Chapter 2 aims to be a practical resource for trainee teachers/teachers, providing an insight into the *Special Educational Needs Code of Practice* guidelines and procedures used in schools to identify and assess pupils who may have special educational needs. The role of the *special educational needs coordinator* will also be discussed.

Chapters 3–9 cover the topics of attention deficit hyperactivity disorder; social, emotional and behavioural difficulties; dyslexia; dyspraxia; autistic spectrum disorder; hearing impairment; and visual impairment. It will be useful to dip in and out of these chapters if you suspect a pupil in your class may have a special educational need in order that you may be able to identify the specific SEN from the guidance provided. These chapters offer top tips for practitioners and lots of strategies when working with pupils with specific SEN.

Going further

References and further reading

DCSF (2007) *Aiming High for Disabled Children: Better Support for Families* www.sourceuk.net/article/9/9894/aiming_high_for_disabled.html, accessed January 2010.

DfES (2009) *Government's strategy for removing barriers to achievement*, http://nationalstrategies.standards.dcsf.gov.uk/node/84379, accessed January 2010.

Parliament UK (2009) *The Warnock Report, 1978*, Select Committee on Education and Skills, http://www.parliament.uk, accessed January 2010.

History of special educational needs/ models of disability

What this chapter will explore:

- Definition of special educational needs (SEN)
- History of SEN
- Medical model of disability and segregation (1870–1970)
- Needs model of disability and integration (1971–1989)
- Social model of disability and inclusion

This chapter will offer a clear definition of special educational needs, along with a brief overview of the history of SEN in the UK. As individuals working with children with SEN, we are not always aware of the theory behind disability and so this chapter is intended to help you understand the medical model of disability, the needs model of disability and integration and the social model of disability.

Definition of special educational needs (SEN)

The Special Educational Needs Code of Practice (*SEN Code*) (DfES, 2001) was introduced to demonstrate the rights and duties introduced by the Special Educational Needs and Disability Act (SENDA) 2001. This code sets out a model of intervention for children with SEN within early education settings and in school settings and provides a toolkit to help practitioners with its implementation.

The law states that if a child has a significantly greater difficulty than most children their age with their schoolwork, communication or behaviour, they have a learning difficulty. According to Directgov (2009) the term SEN refers to 'children who have learning difficulties or disabilities that make it harder for them to learn or access education than most children of the same age.'

The *SEN Code* (DfES, 2001) proposes that children have special educational needs if they have a learning difficulty which calls for special educational provision to be made for them.

Children have a learning difficulty if they:

(a) have a significantly greater difficulty in learning than the majority of children of the same age; or

(b) have a disability which prevents or hinders them from making use of educational facilities of a kind generally provided for children of the same age in schools within the area of the local authority (LA);

(c) are under compulsory school age and fall within the definition at (a) or (b) above or would so do if special educational provision was not made for them. Children must not be regarded as having a learning difficulty solely because the language or form of language of their home is different from the language in which they will be taught.

Special educational provision means:

(a) for children aged two or over, educational provision that is additional to, or otherwise different from, the educational provision made generally for children of their age in schools maintained by the local authority, other than special schools, in the area;

(b) for children under two, educational provision of any kind.

This clear definition of SEN has only been introduced as a result of years of experience working with children with diverse and complex learning difficulties. It provides a framework for the management of inclusion and SEN. The *Code* places a much stronger emphasis on working with parents, pupil participation and working in partnership with other agencies to ensure that children with SEN have a right to be educated in a mainstream school (Directgov, 2009).

The *SEN Code* (DfES, 2001) demonstrates four principle areas of special educational need:

communication and interaction

cognition and learning

behaviour, emotional and social development

sensory and/or physical needs.

UsefulWebsite

http://www.teachernet.gov.uk/doc/3724/SENCodeOfPractice.pdf

This is an excellent website for exploring the *SEN Code* in more detail. You can find out what the *Code* means for children with SEN specifically in relation to provision for education.

History of SEN

The term special educational needs is not new, but has been used to describe learners who have learning difficulties for many years. It is helpful to trace the origins of SEN in order to understand how far policy and practice have developed.

Indeed, when compulsory schooling began in 1870, children with disabilities were seen as unfit to be placed in a mainstream school and remained the responsibility of the health authority. This resulted in children with disabilities being denied the right to education and the activities that would normally be available in the local school. These children were looked upon as deficient, and as a result they were often isolated and rejected by society. This model of disability is the 'medical model', which implies that the disabled person is defined specifically in relation to

Medical model of disability and segregation (1870–1970)

The medical model of disability has had a strong influence on educational provision for children with SEN. When state provision for special education was introduced in the nineteenth century doctors, paediatricians and psychologists were very powerful in the teaching and learning of children with special needs. The role of the medical officers was to identify and place children with special needs within a segregated system (Hodkinson and Vickerman, 2009).

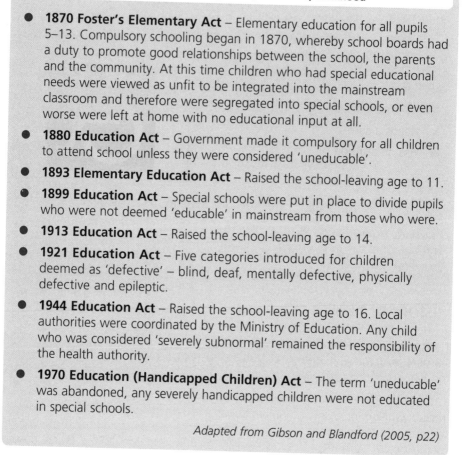

Medical model of disability and segregation (1870–1970) continued

- **1870 Foster's Elementary Act** – Elementary education for all pupils 5–13. Compulsory schooling began in 1870, whereby school boards had a duty to promote good relationships between the school, the parents and the community. At this time children who had special educational needs were viewed as unfit to be integrated into the mainstream classroom and therefore were segregated into special schools, or even worse were left at home with no educational input at all.
- **1880 Education Act** – Government made it compulsory for all children to attend school unless they were considered 'uneducable'.
- **1893 Elementary Education Act** – Raised the school-leaving age to 11.
- **1899 Education Act** – Special schools were put in place to divide pupils who were not deemed 'educable' in mainstream from those who were.
- **1913 Education Act** – Raised the school-leaving age to 14.
- **1921 Education Act** – Five categories introduced for children deemed as 'defective' – blind, deaf, mentally defective, physically defective and epileptic.
- **1944 Education Act** – Raised the school-leaving age to 16. Local authorities were coordinated by the Ministry of Education. Any child who was considered 'severely subnormal' remained the responsibility of the health authority.
- **1970 Education (Handicapped Children) Act** – The term 'uneducable' was abandoned, any severely handicapped children were not educated in special schools.

Adapted from Gibson and Blandford (2005, p22)

their medical condition. The model is based on the view of the disabled person as totally dependent on the medical profession and clearly focuses on sickness rather than health. Central to this approach is a view of the child with special educational needs as 'deficient' (Clough and Corbett, 2000, p12).

This model only disempowers, and uses medical diagnosis to control the individual with the disability; it views the disabled person, not society, as the problem. This model is rejected by disabled people but may sometimes permeate attitudes towards disabled people in general.

Over the years the structure of education has changed significantly. In 1944 the Education Act was passed, which gave local authorities the responsibility of making a decision with regard to individual children with special educational needs and whether they required special educational treatment. This integrated approach began to emerge and the 'needs model' of disability was introduced.

This model of disability moved away from segregating children and placed emphasis on the individual needs of the child.

- Housebound
- Confined to a wheelchair
- Needs a doctor
- Needs a cure
- Has an attitude

Fig 1.1: Medical model of disability

Why not try this?

Consider the following questions in light of the medical model of disability:

- Do you feel sorry for an individual with a disability?
- Do you feel you want to help the individual?
- Do you know how to talk to an individual with a disability?

Needs model of disability and integration (1971–1989)

- **1976 Education Act** – Children were no longer selected by ability for secondary education.
- **1978 Warnock Report** – All categories of handicap abolished and replaced with a spectrum of SEN, and greater parental involvement encouraged. Five-stage recognition and assessment of needs introduced.
- **1981 Education Act 'Special Educational Needs'** – This was a key policy whereby Warnock's recommendations were established.
- **1988 Education Reform Act** – National Curriculum introduced. All pupils regardless of their needs/disabilities entitled to access the National Curriculum.

Adapted from Gibson and Blandford (2005, p2)

| Why not try this? |

Reflect on the ways in which you consider that practice towards the education of children with SEN has changed over the years. Consider this question in light of the above timeline of changes in SEN policies.

The needs model of disability

The Warnock Report (1978) is a landmark for SEN and the education of children with disabilities. It was following this report that the term *special educational needs* was introduced into UK legislation. The report emphasised two categories of children with SEN: those children who experienced difficulty at school whose needs could be met at the mainstream school; and those children who as a result of more complex learning difficulties were not able to have their needs met at the mainstream school and would require specialised educational environments.

| Why not try this? |

Reflect on the impact that the Warnock Report has had on the inclusion of children with SEN. How has policy changed over time? What effect may this have on practice?

Following the Warnock Report, the 1981 Education Act 'Special Educational Needs' was introduced, which established Warnock's recommendations. This was the most significant Act to be introduced as it resulted in a change of emphasis with regard to children with SEN. Children with special educational needs were now offered the right to mainstream education, rather than being segregated, which demonstrates a clear move towards inclusion. Teachers were at this time given responsibilities in relation to the identification and assessment of children who they suspected may have special educational needs.

Another major shift towards inclusive education was the Education Reform Act, introduced in 1988. This Act identified a requirement for all children to have a right to a 'balanced and broadly based curriculum which is relevant to their individual needs' (OPSI) (Office of Public Sector Information, 2008).

The Education Reform Act was a turning point and the 'social model' of disability began to emerge.

It is evident from this model of disability (and see Figure 1.2) that the emphasis is placed on the disabling environment rather than the individual. This model demonstrates a clear move towards an inclusive education for children with special educational needs, as the responsibility lies with the primary or secondary school to adapt its environment and policy to fit the pupil's needs. This is in contrast to the medical model, which views the child with SEN as 'uneducable'.

UsefulWebsite

http://www.publications.parliament.uk/pa/cm200506/cmselect/
cmeduski/478/47805.htm

This website will enable you to find out about the history of SEN and the impact of the Warnock Report on children with special educational needs.

The 1993 Education Act marked a shift towards inclusion with the introduction of new elements, including the setting up of the SEN Tribunal and *The Code of Practice on the Identification and Assessment of Special Educational Needs* (DfE, 1994).

UsefulWebsite

http://www.opsi.gov.uk/acts/acts1988/ukpga_19880040_en_1

This is an excellent website that offers a full description of the Education Reform Act and the duties of the Act with respect to the National Curriculum.

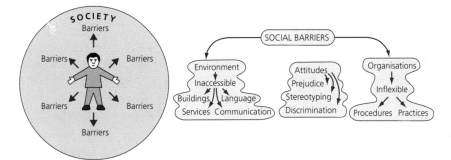

Fig 1.2: The Social Model of Disability

Social model of disability and inclusion

● **1993 Education Act** – The aim of this Act was to increase the quality, diversity, autonomy and accountability of schools and to extend parental choice. Class teachers were at this time responsible for SEN at the early stages.

Social model of disability and inclusion continued

- **1994 Code of Practice: Identification and Assessment of Special Educational Needs** – Class teachers no longer responsible for SEN at the early stages, as the role of the **Special Educational Needs Coordinator (SENCO)** was made statutory. All schools must have a SENCO and this role involved coordination of provision for pupils with SEN.

- **1995 Disability Discrimination Act (DDA)** – This law strengthened the rights of disabled people, as it became unlawful to discriminate against disabled people in connection with employment, the provision of goods, facilities and services or the disposal or management of premises. However, it failed to take education into account.

- **1996 Education Act** – Identified children as having special educational needs if they had a learning difficulty significantly greater than the majority of those of the same age (OPSI, 1996).

- **1997 Green Paper: Excellence for All Children** – Introduced with a view to more inclusive education, the emphasis was placed on collaborative practice between mainstream and special schools.

- **1998 White Paper: Meeting Special Educational Needs: A Programme of Action** – This paper formed the basis from which the *Special Educational Needs Code of Practice* emerged.

- **2001: Special Educational Needs and Disability Act** – This extended the Disability Discrimination Act to include education. The duties of this Act make it unlawful to discriminate against pupils with disabilities in respect of all aspects of their school life.

- **2003 Every Child Matters: Change for Children** – A government strategy introduced with regard to ensuring the well-being of children and young people from birth to age 19.

Adapted from Gibson and Blandford (2005, p3)

Following this, the *SEN Code* was introduced in 2001 to provide practical advice to local authorities and schools to ensure that the correct procedures for identification, assessment and provision were followed with regard to children with SEN. This *Code* was welcomed by parents as the guidelines highlight that parents have the right to choose a mainstream education for their child with SEN and, if this choice is made, the education service is under obligation to do everything possible to provide the necessary support in order that the child may access mainstream education (GovernorNet, 2008). An article published by the *Guardian* highlights the negative impact of the statutory framework for identifying and meeting children's special educational needs (http://www.guardian.co.uk/education/2002/jun/21/schools.uk1/print).

UsefulWebsite

http://www.everychildmatters.gov.uk/news/?asset=News&id=33739

This website offers an overview of the background to Every Child Matters and the aims and purposes of this agenda. On the website you will be able to search for guidance in relation to meeting the needs of the individual child.

The impact of the Every Child Matters (ECM) agenda has been significant, as it advocates a multi-agency approach to ensuring that the needs of children with SEN are met. The focus of ECM is to ensure inclusive lifelong learning opportunities for all children, ensuring that every aspect of school life is taken into consideration.

Conclusion

As practitioners and educators it is important that we are aware of the history of SEN in order that we can move forward in an ever-changing society and make a positive contribution to the lives of children with SEN. We have come a long way by understanding the radical changes in policy and practice, which have a substantial impact on the education of children with special educational needs. When making decisions about a child's special educational need this will help us to gain a better understanding of the SEN legislation that governs the UK.

Key ideas summary

- Think about what you have learned about the definition of 'special educational needs'.
- What is a SEN?
- Reflect on the history of SEN – what impact have government policies and reports had on SEN since 1870?
- Consider the medical model of disability and the social model of disability. What effects would each have on the individual with special educational needs?

Going further

References and further reading

Clough, P. and Corbett, J. (2000) *Theories of Inclusive Education: A Student's Guide*, London: Sage.

Cowne, E. (2003) The SENCO *Handbook: Working within a Whole-school Approach*, (4th Edn), London: Fulton.

DfE (1994) *The Code of Practice on the Identification and Assessment of Special Educational Needs*, London: HMSO.

DfES (2001) *The Special Educational Needs Code of Practice*, Nottingham: DfES, http://www.teachernet.gov.uk/_doc/3724/SENCodeOfPractice.pdf.

Directgov (2009) http://www.direct.gov.uk/en/Parents/Schoolslearninganddevelopment/SpecialEducationalNeeds/DG_4008600, accessed January 2009.

Dyson, A. and Millward, A. (2000) *Schools and Special Needs: Issues of Innovation and Inclusion*, London: Sage.

Gibson, S. and Blandford, S. (2005) *Managing Special Educational Needs: A Practical Guide for Primary and Secondary Schools*, London: Sage.

GovernorNet (2008) *Children with Special Educational Needs: Overview*, http://www.governornet.co.uk/cropArticle.cfm?topicAreaId=1&contentId=275&mode=bg.

Hodkinson, A. and Vickerman, P. (2009) *Key Issues in Educational Needs and Inclusion*, London: Sage.

OPSI (1996) *Education Act 1996*, http://www.opsi.gov.uk/ACTS/acts1996/ukpga_19960056_en_1, accessed January 2009.

OPSI (2008) *Education Reform Act 1988,* http://www.opsi.gov.uk/acts/acts1988/ukpga_19880040_en_1.

OPSI (2010) http://www.opsi.gov.uk/acts/acts1988/ukpga_19880040_en_1.

SENDA (2001) Special Educational Needs and Disability Act 2001, available from http://www.opsi.gov.uk/Acts, accessed January 2009.

Teachernet (2008) National Curriculum, http://www.teachernet.gov.uk/management/atoz/n/nationalcurriculum/

Identification of SEN and the role of the special educational needs coordinator

What this chapter will explore:

- *SEN Code* guidelines regarding SEN
- Identification of pupils with SEN
- Procedures for identifying and assessing pupils with SEN in mainstream schools (School Action/School Action Plus)
- The future role of the SENCO

This chapter will provide an overview of the *Special Educational Needs Code of Practice* (DfES, 2001) guidelines for identifying and assessing pupils with SEN. As educators we will all, at some time in our career, work with a child who we identify as having special educational needs and this chapter is intended to help you gain an insight into the procedures used in schools for identifying and assessing SEN pupils and to provide an overview of the role of the special educational needs coordinator. This is key to the successful inclusion of pupils with SEN in mainstream schools.

SEN Code guidelines regarding SEN

As outlined in Chapter 1, the Education Act 1996 identified children as having special educational needs if they had a learning difficulty significantly greater than the majority of those of the same age (OPSI, 1996). The *SEN Code* reinforced this, stating:

● A child with special educational needs should have their needs met.
● The special educational needs of children will normally be met in mainstream schools or settings.
● The views of the child should be sought and taken into account.
● Parents have a vital role to play in supporting their children's education.
● Children with special educational needs should be offered full access to a broad, balanced and relevant education, including an appropriate curriculum for the foundation stage and the National Curriculum.

UsefulWebsite

http://www.opsi.gov.uk/ACTS/acts1996/ukpga_19960056_en_1

This website is useful as it offers the contents of the 1996 Education Act and may act as a guideline with regard to statutory education. It will be helpful specifically for finding out about the requirements of the Act.

Identification of pupils with SEN

Every school and early years setting must have a SENCO, and the SENCO has a vital role to play in ensuring that the provision for all children with SEN is suitable and offers an inclusive approach. This role will be discussed in more depth later in the chapter. Children who attend primary schools may already have been identified as having special educational needs if they have attended a nursery prior to primary school; but this is not always the case.

Early educational settings are required to keep records of attainment of every child who attends and these are a useful way of identifying if a child has a special educational need on entry to the primary phase of education. LAs use a one-off baseline assessment that is conducted very soon after the child starts primary school, and this should highlight any areas for concern and ensure that teachers are watchful and able to identify those children with special educational needs as a result (DfES, 2001, p44). This assessment is used in order to assess children and plan for their future education and also to provide a means for measuring their future education.

Reflecting on practice

Gary has just started primary school and is finding it very difficult to follow instructions. Prior to primary school Gary attended a nursery; however, there has been no indication from the notes forwarded to the primary school that Gary has any learning difficulties or behavioural problems. At primary school it has become apparent that Gary is easily distracted and is unable to concentrate for more than a few minutes at a time.

Gary is demonstrating signs of difficulty when writing. He is unable to write his own name, whereas the other children in his class are able to complete this task. When Gary is asked to carry out any tasks that involve reading or writing he starts to misbehave and make silly noises to avoid completing the work.

The teacher is very concerned following the baseline assessment, as Gary, it appears, is operating well below his own age of five.

Consider the following:

1. What steps would you take following the baseline assessment and your observation of Gary's inability to read and write?

2. What action would you take if you identified a child with problems similar to Gary's?

3. Who would you inform of your concerns?

TOP TIP!

Every time inappropriate behaviour commences make a note of what occurred prior to the behaviour and how the behaviour exhibits itself. This will help you identify the key times when the behaviour is being displayed and whether it occurs in a specific environment.

From the case study about Gary it is evident that the nursery school he attended failed to forward any notes to the primary school regarding the behaviour he exhibited. How do you feel the teacher may have benefited from having this information from the onset?

Procedures for identifying and assessing pupils with SEN in mainstream schools (School Action/ School Action Plus)

School Action is an intervention and support strategy where evidence exists to suggest that a child is not making progress and there is a need for action to meet the individual learning difficulties of the child. This may result in intervention and assessment by the class teacher and the SENCO in order to develop an **individual education plan** (IEP) which is an individualised plan with set targets that are reviewed termly. The pupil at this time will remain in the mainstream classroom, with flexible grouping arrangements in the classroom. The main provision will be provided by the teacher, and the SENCO will be involved in target setting and assessment of the pupil. Some support may be offered from the teaching assistant in the class.

The following triggers for intervention through School Action are suggested within the *SEN Code*:

- makes little or no progress even when teaching approaches are targeted in a child's area of weakness;
- shows signs of difficulty in developing literacy or mathematics skills that result in poor attainment in some curriculum areas;
- presents persistent emotional or behavioural difficulties that are not ameliorated by the behaviour management techniques usually employed in the school;
- has sensory or physical problems, and continues to make little or no progress despite the provision of specialist equipment;
- has communication and/or interaction difficulties and continues to make little or no progress despite the provision of a differentiated curriculum.

School Action Plus involves external services in the planning and assessment of the individual education plan targets. Targets are set and reviewed at agreed intervals and parents are involved in the short- and long-term planning and implementation of the targets. The pupil will be based predominantly in the mainstream classroom, with flexible grouping arrangements and direct support in a small group or at times individually to support his/her IEP targets. The main provision will be provided by the class teacher and there will be some direct support from the SENCO, teacher or learning support assistant providing individual or small group tuition.

The following triggers for intervention through School Action Plus are suggested within the *SEN Code*:

● continues to make little or no progress in specific areas over a long period;

● continues working at National Curriculum levels substantially below that expected of children of a similar age;

● continues to have difficulty in developing literacy and mathematics skills;

● has emotional or behavioural difficulties that substantially and regularly interfere with the child's own learning or that of the class group, despite having an individualised behaviour programme;

● has sensory or physical needs and requires additional specialist equipment or regular advice or visits by a specialist service;

● has ongoing communication or interaction difficulties that impede the development of social relationships and cause substantial barriers to learning.

It is vital that the identification of pupils who may have special educational needs is made as early as possible. Once the pupil has been identified action may be taken and strategies put in place to meet the individual needs of the pupil. SENCOs play a vital role in advising and supporting staff in planning and meeting the needs of learners with SEN.

TOP TIP!

If you suspect that a child in your class has special educational needs, it is a good idea to note down each time you feel the child struggles with a particular task. This will enable you to form a clear picture of the child and offer evidence when identifying a special educational need.

If a class teacher or SENCO identifies that a pupil may have a special educational need the first step is to intervene and provide support that is additional to or different from the support already in place. Intervention of this nature may be as a result of a concern raised by the class teacher or other member of staff about a child who, despite receiving additional or differentiated learning opportunities, targeting their specific weakness, still appears to make little or no progress. This stage of intervention is termed School Action, described earlier in the chapter.

The SENCO and teacher at this point will decide on the action required to assist the child with progression. An example of this may be by offering different learning materials or specialist equipment to meet the individual child's needs, or offering some kind of individual support (DfES, 2001).

If, following this intervention, the child fails to make progress it may be that a request for help from external services is required. This procedure is carried out through School Action Plus, whereby at a review meeting with parents a decision is taken to bring in outside specialists to measure the child's progress with a view to providing the necessary support to enable the child to continue in a mainstream educational environment. At this point the SENCO, class teacher and external support services work together to produce a new individual education plan, which should be implemented in the normal classroom and offers clear strategies for meeting the individual needs of the pupil (DfES, 2001).

If this action fails to assist the individual pupil in making progress, there may be a request for a statutory assessment by a school to the local authority. It is the responsibility of the school to offer evidence of the child's progress over time and attempt to offer support in order to deal with the individual special educational needs prior to a **Statement of Special Educational Needs** being issued by the local authority. If and when a Statement of SEN is issued, it is the responsibility of the local authority to consider whether the individual child's needs can be met at a mainstream school and, at this point, the child may be transferred to a special school if appropriate. It will now be useful to consider the role of the SENCO as this is crucial to the success of the pupil with SEN.

Reflecting on practice

A day in the life of a SENCO

Melanie Coultas, SENCO at a Derbyshire mainstream secondary school, shares her experience of the varied role of the SENCO. On a daily basis Melanie is responsible for the coordination and teaching of any literacy support that is required for pupils with special educational needs. This has an impact on the number of staff required and Melanie has to manage teachers and teaching assistants in relation to literacy support, in order that they are aware of the individual needs of the pupils to be taught. Melanie also has to liaise with colleagues throughout the school and advise them with regard to all aspects of the curriculum design and delivery in order that the most effective teaching approaches are adopted for pupils with SEN. Melanie also encourages all members of staff to recognise and fulfil their statutory responsibilities to pupils with SEN. It is also essential that provision for pupils with SEN is in line with the Every Child Matters Agenda and this is also the responsibility of the SENCO. Melanie is also involved in communicating with and supporting parents of pupils with special educational needs. Melanie

→

is tasked with collating and writing annual review reports focusing on progression and raising achievement, and she also has to oversee confidential reports written by external agencies that will inform the support offered to the SEN pupil attending a mainstream school.

In Melanie's experience as a SENCO in a secondary school, it is rare that pupils are identified as having a SEN at this stage. Predominantly, the pupil would have been identified prior to attending secondary school (while at primary school). Pupils are withdrawn from modern foreign language groups if they have a reading age two years or more below their chronological age (based on reading tests completed in October of Year 6 at primary school). A nurture group is set up for the most vulnerable pupils, which takes place six weeks prior to the summer holidays and during the first half-term of the school year. Melanie is enthused by the impact this has had on the pupils, as some of the group have already gained the confidence to go to lessons rather than attend the nurture group. Additionally, all Year 7 pupils are screened for spelling in September to check for possible dyslexia, and following this, if required, further testing and interventions take place. During the first two weeks of term every teaching assistant is allocated to Year 7 form groups and remains with the group for the whole year. They were able to identify pupils who may require additional help at a very early stage. In future, all pupils will be tested in September and any students who require literacy support will be withdrawn for additional literacy support. These support mechanisms ensure that pupils are assessed and identified at a very early stage with a view to offering support wherever necessary.

Prior to the Special Educational Needs and Disability Act 2001 the role of the SENCO did not exist. At this time it was the responsibility of the remedial teacher to support children with special educational needs and ensure that their individual needs were met as far as possible.

SENCOs were introduced in order to reduce the barriers to learning that children with SEN may face in the mainstream school environment.

The future role of the SENCO

Special educational needs coordinators play a key role in ensuring that schools meet the needs of children and young people with SEN and disabilities. With this in mind the Department for Children, Schools and Families have introduced a new requirement for SENCOs to be qualified teachers, in order that a SENCO is able to influence differentiated teaching and learning matched to pupils' individual needs

(DCSF, 2009). The new regulations were implemented from 1 September 2009, but will allow a two-year transitional period for SENCOs not currently teachers to gain Qualified Teacher Status by September 2011 (DCSF, 2009).

Why not try this?

Think about your own practice and reflect on the following:

- What does the role of the SENCO involve?
- How much contact have you had with the SENCO in your school?
- What steps have you both taken to make sure that pupils with SEN have been supported in the classroom?
- What could you do to ensure that you work together with the SENCO to provide an effective environment for the pupil with SEN?

Conclusion

The role of the SENCO will evolve over time. By ensuring that the individual needs of the pupil with SEN are identified and assessed at an early stage of their education it is more likely that each individual with SEN will have a better chance of achieving his/her educational goals.

Key ideas summary

- Think about what you have learned about identifying pupils with SEN in mainstream schools.
- What are the *Special Educational Needs Code of Practice* guidelines for identifying SEN pupils?
- What are the stages of intervention used when identifying a pupil with SEN?
- What is the most important role of the SENCO in ensuring the needs of pupils with SEN are met?

Going further

References and further reading

Cowne, E. (2008) *The SENCO Handbook: Working Within a Whole-school Approach*, Abingdon: David Fulton.

DCSF (2009) The Education (Special Educational Needs Co-ordinators) (England) Regulations, 2008 (2008 No. 2945), http://www.teachernet.gov.uk/wholeschool/sen/teacherlearningassistant/sencos2008/, accessed January 2009.

DfES (2001) *The Special Educational Needs Code of Practice*, Nottingham: DfES.

Dyson, A. and Millward, A. (2000) *Schools and Special Needs: Issues of Innovation and Inclusion*, London: Sage.

OPSI (1996) *Education Act 1996*, http://www.opsi.gov.uk/ACTS/acts1996/ukpga_19960056_en_1, accessed January 2009.

Teachernet (2009) *Special Educational Needs Identification and Assessment,* http://www.teachernet.gov.uk/management/atoz/s/senidentificationandassessment/, accessed January 2009.

Teachernet (2009) *SENCO Job Description*, http://www.teachernet.gov.uk/management/staffingandprofessionaldevelopment/jobdescriptions/senco/, accessed January 2009.

Attention deficit hyperactivity disorder

What this chapter will explore:

- What is attention deficit hyperactivity disorder (ADHD)?
- What are the signs of ADHD? (key characteristics)
- Controversies surrounding the treatment of ADHD with medication
- Identifying ADHD in the classroom
- Pupils with ADHD in mainstream and special schools
- Factors to consider when working with pupils with ADHD
- A framework for collaborative working
- The systemic analysis model
- Strategies for working with children with ADHD in the classroom

This chapter will give you an overview of the key characteristics of ADHD. As individuals, we may all present one or more of the symptoms of ADHD

through childhood and during adulthood; however, these symptoms are only considered abnormal when they are excessive. This chapter is intended to help you identify a child with ADHD, help you understand the possible causes of their behaviour and adopt strategies you can introduce in your own classroom to help both you and the child work and learn together more effectively.

No matter how experienced you are at working with children, this will not prepare you when you are faced with a child with ADHD, who can and will cause chaos, especially when faced with a new environment and a teacher who is clearly inexperienced in dealing with their specific needs. This chapter will help you to understand the complexity of ADHD and I hope as a result you will feel more confident when working with children with the condition.

What is ADHD?

Attention deficit hyperactivity disorder, otherwise known as ADHD, was first diagnosed by the American Psychiatric Association in 1994 (APA, 1994).

There are three diagnostic criteria: **inattention, impulsiveness**, and **hyperactivity**, which manifest themselves in excess when compared with peers. These must have been present for at least six months to an extent that is disruptive and inappropriate for the developmental level in order for the child to gain a diagnosis of ADHD.

Between 3 and 6 per cent of school-aged children are affected by ADHD (Tannock, 1998) a condition that makes learning difficult. This means that the average UK classroom will include at least one child with ADHD. Although children during early infancy sometimes display symptoms of ADHD, diagnosis is predominantly between the ages of three and four (Anastopolous, 1999).

What are the signs of ADHD? (key characteristics)

Children with ADHD often display different characteristics of the condition. However, as a general rule the following behavioural and attentional difficulties are the most common in the classroom:

- unable to focus on details

- easily distracted
- talk excessively
- frequently interrupt others
- appear disorganised and forgetful
- demonstrate difficulties in sustaining attention to tasks and fail to complete them.

Let's look in more detail at the key characteristics of ADHD.

Inattentiveness

When working with children who demonstrate the symptoms of ADHD, it is noticeable that the child will predominantly have great difficulty in concentrating on educational tasks and may be inclined to move from one task to another, quickly losing motivation if they consider the task boring. This was highlighted when working with a young person with ADHD recently. It soon became apparent that this pupil found it very difficult to stay on task for more than a few minutes and as a result she distracted other pupils by ripping up paper and throwing it around the room. She also used to tap the desk when she was finding it hard to concentrate on the set task.

It is important to mention that when the child is receiving individual attention, he/she is able to stay on task for quite some time. When working with the pupil I have just mentioned, if she had my attention she worked very well indeed. However, as soon as I diverted my attention to another pupil, she became agitated and her behaviour would be very inappropriate. For a task to be of interest to the child it is necessary that the subject area motivates the child with ADHD, as without this motivation there may be consequences, specifically in relation to the behaviour the child may display. These may include distracting other children in the classroom, disrupting work and attention-seeking behaviour such as shouting, making noises and banging on tables. This behaviour may present challenges for the teacher/practitioner specifically as regards ensuring that other children's learning is not affected.

Impulsiveness

Prior to diagnosis, children with ADHD may often be referred to as 'naughty' as they will act without reflection or consideration of the consequences (Wender, 2000). For example, when playing a game the child with ADHD finds it difficult to wait his/her turn and may 'push in'; during discussion time they may even shout out the answers, appearing very attention seeking. There is much controversy with regard to the term ADHD, and many individuals will suggest that children with ADHD are just misbehaving.

Hyperactivity

Children with ADHD often display signs of hyperactivity, including behaviours such as hand/foot tapping, talking excessively, and a lack of ability to sit still for more than a few seconds at a time. We need to be aware that not all children with ADHD are hyperactive, some children may only have problems with inattention, but many may have a combination of all three types of problem.

Research evidence

These are three theoretical explanations of ADHD (Tannock, 1998, cited in Hughes and Cooper, 2007, p6):

- **cognitive** explanation – underlying problem is linked to a dysfunctional response inhibition system;
- cognitive neuroscientific approach – family environmental factors may be in part a contributory factor;
- genetic approach – ADHD may be a result of abnormalities in the **dopamine** system.

Reflecting on practice

Keely's mother is concerned that, during school hours, Keely is always at the centre of any problem, and even though she is not always involved, she always gets the blame.

Mother: She always speaks out and interrupts when the teacher is trying to sort out a problem. One example was at school, there was a fight during break time which was nothing to do with Keely, but as she was in the location at the time, she got the blame. She always shouts at the teacher as she is not able to keep her thoughts to herself and this results in problems.

Keely's mother is of the opinion that Keely lacks confidence and as a result she is melodramatic in order to receive attention. Keely is unable to explain her behaviour, although she is aware that she has regular outbursts and is unable to control these.

Keely: I'm always in trouble, I threw a chair across the room once because I didn't think it fair that we had to do more maths work when it's boring. Jamie was getting all the attention because he can't do the work.

Keely believes her actions are reasonable as she feels that she has been treated unfairly. →

This case study highlights the issues that a child with ADHD may face in school. It is clear from the behaviour exhibited by Keely that she is very unhappy with the environment she works in at school. She may feel excluded from the educational environment due to her ADHD and find it difficult to cope in this setting.

Consider the following:

1. Have you come across children with personalities similar to Keely's in your class?

2. How have you reacted to this child?

3. How do you feel you could deal with the situation differently to produce a positive working environment?

Controversies surrounding the treatment of ADHD with medication

Research evidence

- Teeter (1998, cited in Hughes and Cooper, 2007) suggests that 'Stimulant medication for children with ADHD' has been at the centre of research as there is much controversy surrounding the issue of giving medication to children with behavioural problems.

- Psycho-stimulants (otherwise known as Ritalin) stimulate brain activity, in particular they increase the effective use by the brain of neurotransmitters. This improves alertness but only for a period of three to four hours. Barkley (1998, cited in Hughes and Cooper, 2007) suggests that Ritalin reduces the symptoms of ADHD in 70–90 per cent of diagnosed children. Although it controls the symptoms of ADHD, this is only a short-term fix. There is much concern about the side effects of Ritalin, which include headaches, stomach ache, difficulty in sleeping, motor and visual tics and suppression of height and weight in some children (Schachar et al., 1997, cited in Hughes and Cooper, 2007, p27).

- Rose (2004, cited in Hughes and Cooper, 2007, p28) agrees with this notion, suggesting that the medication for the treatment of ADHD may be a limited fix as it can control some of the core symptoms of ADHD over a short period of time but has limited efficacy over time.

It is useful when considering the implications of teaching a pupil with ADHD to address the question 'Is controlling the symptoms of ADHD the most effective way of managing the individual behaviours of the child?' I would like to draw on my own experience regarding this controversial issue to demonstrate the reality of the situation.

Why not try this?

In view of these research findings, what are your opinions on using Ritalin to control the inappropriate behaviours of individuals who have ADHD? Consider the side effects of Ritalin and its usefulness in providing effective treatment of ADHD.

Reflecting on practice

While recently teaching a pupil with ADHD, my ultimate goal was to ensure that I implemented strategies for preventing and managing inappropriate behaviour and promoted positive behaviour in the classroom. Ben was taking Ritalin on a daily basis, and although the 'quick fix' was apparent when he had just taken the medication, it was also apparent that when the effects of the drug were wearing off Ben found it very hard to work in a classroom situation as the ADHD symptoms seemed to be exacerbated during this period.

At these times, Ben's behaviour became very aggressive and had a profound effect both on himself and the remainder of the pupils in the class. He would often pick up a chair and throw it across the room and resort to very aggressive behaviour towards both staff and other pupils. The only time this behaviour did not occur was when he was involved in sporting activities as this was something that particularly motivated him.

In cases like Ben's it is important to realise that the ultimate goals of intervention for pupils with ADHD are not just to control the symptoms, but to ensure that the individual needs of the pupil are understood and met in order to facilitate educational progress in a meaningful way that will be of maximum benefit to the individual. Strategies for meeting the needs of pupils with ADHD will be addressed later in this chapter.

Identifying ADHD in the classroom

In your career you will inevitably come across a child with the symptoms of ADHD. In the classroom, there may be two children who always pay attention to someone or something they shouldn't be, they are easily distracted and never stay on task for more than a few minutes, often fidgeting and moving around in search of distraction. Some children with ADHD may be able to pay attention for a short time, but this is intermittent unless the child is very interested in the subject area, whereas other ADHD children may not be able to pay attention to one thing at one time and may become very easily distracted.

These children often shout out in class and other children can feel very intimidated by their actions. This was true of a pupil with ADHD who I taught recently. She would talk above everyone else in the class, and if another pupil was asked to answer a question she would immediately shout out the answer. She rarely considered the consequences prior to taking action, which often caused problems as she would strike another child without thinking about the consequences; and she needed constant reassurance regarding her work and behaviour in order to ensure she reacted in a positive way.

Reflecting on practice

Charles continually bumps into children accidently and yesterday a child was elbowed and became very upset as a result. The teacher explained to Charles that this behaviour was not acceptable, by telling Charles how the other child feels. The teacher did this by saying 'I will say it first, then you can say it. I don't like it when you hit me like that, it hurt.' Charles repeated the words and the other child involved then apologised too. Following this intervention, the children became friends again.

Consider the following:

1. Have you come across children like Charles in your class?
2. How have you reacted to this child?
3. How do you feel you could deal with the situation differently to produce a positive working environment?

A child with ADHD may also display extreme reactions when sad, happy, excited, and will constantly be seeking positive reinforcement for any work they are doing. An example of extreme reaction may be when the child with ADHD blurts out the answers all the time as a way of seeking attention. In order to overcome this problem, positive reinforcement is the best behavioural management strategy to use to build the confidence of a child with ADHD. The teacher/practitioner may recognise and praise specific instances when the child carries out a task correctly:

'I like the way Keely remembers to put her hand up and waits to be called on. Thank you, Keely.'

This will reinforce the good behaviour of the child and also raise their self-esteem when they recognise they are doing what is expected of them.

Children who have ADHD predominantly have trouble staying on task, staying seated, and many may be immature developmentally, educationally and/or socially. When working with pupils with ADHD it is important to recognise that they find it very difficult to sit still for long periods of time.

TOP TIP!

When working with a child who displays signs of ADHD you may find it more appropriate to let the pupil wander around the classroom in a controlled way wherever possible, as by restricting the pupil you will only add to their anxiety level.

Top tips for identifying ADHD

● Can the child pay attention in class?

● Is the child impulsive? Does he/she call out in class? Does he/she bother other children with his/her impulsiveness?

● Does the child have trouble staying seated?

● Does the child often get in fights?

● Can the child wait his/her turn in a line, or to answer a question?

● Is the child calm?

● Does the child stay on task well or does he/she fidget a lot?

● Does the child lack awareness of personal space?

● Does the child seem to be immature developmentally, educationally or socially?

UsefulWebsite

http://www.adhd.org.uk/

This is an excellent website for ADHD – specifically for getting ideas about how to manage the condition. There is detailed information about ADHD and the treatment used to overcome problems faced by the individual with ADHD. There are also personal stories written by people with ADHD.

TOP TIP!

If you suspect that a child has ADHD it may be a good idea to note down each time the behaviour discussed here occurs, how often it occurs and what the circumstances are. This will enable you to form a clear picture of the child and identify whether the child needs referral to a specialist in order for diagnosis to take place.

UsefulWebsite

http://www.teachernet.gov.uk/_doc/3724/SENCodeOfPractice.pdf

This website offers a comprehensive guide to the Special Educational Needs and Disabilities Act 2001, which you will find useful when working with pupils who you suspect have special educational needs. This website offers practical advice to local authorities on carrying out their statutory duties to identify, assess and make provision for children's special educational needs.

Pupils with ADHD in mainstream and special needs schools

As outlined in Chapter 2, under the terms of the Special Educational Needs and Disability Act 2001, all children between the ages of 4 and 19 in the UK have the right to be educated in a mainstream school regardless of special educational needs or disabilities. In reality this is not the case: approximately 7 per cent of children are educated in the private sector; 2 per cent of children being educated in specialist provision, including special schools and pupil referral units, young offenders' institutions and medical facilities (Hughes and Cooper, 2007, p40).

Children with ADHD should have the opportunity to reach their maximum potential, and thus should be given a choice of educational setting in order that they may engage actively and constructively in the social and academic life of the institution. If the mainstream school is able to meet the needs of the child who has ADHD, this is considered appropriate; however, alternative methods such as special schools may be preferred. Hughes and Cooper (2007) advocate that effective education relies heavily on the setting in which the student is learning and is dependent on their social, emotional and learning needs being met.

Failure to meet these needs may result in the child suffering from social exclusion, and in turn may affect their academic achievement. It is important to recognise that if the pupil is being taught in a mainstream environment, all staff need to be aware of what strategies are in place in order to provide consistency for the pupil, as failure to do this will only exacerbate the difficulties faced by the pupil even further.

Factors to consider when working with pupils with ADHD

When working with pupils with ADHD, there are many factors to consider:

● Training and knowledge about ADHD – Teachers need to be aware that children with ADHD are not 'naughty children' and their actions are not directed at teachers personally. The behaviours displayed are a result of physiological and biological deficiencies. It is important to gain an understanding of the condition in order that the challenging behaviours are dealt with in an appropriate way.

● Communication between home and school – Regular and effective communication is of paramount importance in order that a good relationship is established between parents and school. This will highlight any issues that arise and may reduce the risk of further problems.

● You need to ensure a clear and structured approach:
  – The pupil with ADHD needs to have a structured approach in order to minimise disruption.
  – They need clear communication, expectations, consequences and feedback.
  – When structuring tasks, consideration should be given to the length of time the task will take, and the need for breaking the task into sizeable chunks.
  – Clear instructions are essential in order that the child with ADHD does not become anxious.
  – The tasks set need to be of interest to the child in order that they do not become bored and, as a result, disruptive.

● Teacher–pupil engagement with tasks:
  – Tasks set need to involve the children with ADHD interacting with their peers, in order to keep them engaged and motivated. An example of good practice would be to involve the child in choosing a game to play with a friend, or using the computer with a friend at break time.
  – Giving the child who has ADHD a responsibility, such as classroom monitor (tidying up books and resources) assists in keeping their attention, as they have a sense of purpose. Provide opportunities for children to demonstrate their strengths to peers.

Top tips for teachers/practitioners

- Understand that not all children with ADHD are hyperactive.
- Don't dismiss the behaviours as poor parenting or poor classroom management.
- Communicate with parents face to face to gain a better understanding of the needs of the child with ADHD.
- Be aware that the child who has ADHD works very well in a one-to-one situation.
- Be aware of the classroom environment; there are many distractions, and rules that may be very difficult for the child with ADHD.

A framework for collaborative working

In order to meet the social, emotional and academic needs of the child with ADHD it is imperative that professionals and parents work together to provide effective strategies to support the child. Burrows and Tamblyn (1980, cited in Hughes and Cooper, 2007) identify a problem-based model, which seeks to encourage a collaborative approach to problem solving (see Figure 3.1).

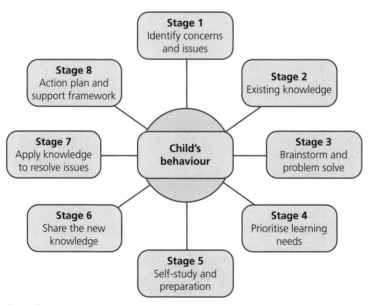

Fig 3.1: The eight-stage problem-based model (Burrows and Tamblyn, 1980, cited Hughes and Cooper, 2007, p61)

Problem-based model

- **Stage 1 Identify concerns** – Collaboration between group members in order to identify each concern – this may be achieved by each group member observing behaviours and making notes in order to identify behaviours.

- **Stage 2 Existing knowledge** – Draw on existing knowledge and consider each concern to clarify any experience of concerns raised – this relies on experienced teachers/practitioners drawing on their knowledge of children with ADHD and relating to this in order to aid them in their identification of children who have ADHD.

- **Stage 3 Problem solve** – Discuss the concerns in order to identify any gaps in knowledge; this will help to resolve the problems by creating new ideas. Highlight key categories – this stage should involve the SENCO and any members of staff working with the child who has ADHD brainstorming in order to obtain a clear understanding of the problems that arise in relation to the individual child with ADHD.

- **Stage 4 Prioritise learning needs** – Prioritise categories to be explored. Agree on learning objectives – this stage should involve staff members agreeing on the individual learning needs of the child with ADHD.

- **Stage 5 Self-study and preparation** – Greater understanding and clarification of concerns may be achieved by all group members or individual members – collaborative working will ensure that all members of staff working with the child who has ADHD will feel supported and will share any concerns in order to aid understanding of any specific issues in relation to the child.

- **Stage 6 Share the new knowledge** – All group members should share any new knowledge in order that the whole group have a better understanding of the knowledge gained – this should occur on a daily basis in order that a full picture is gained and staff are better equipped to deal with the child who has ADHD.

- **Stage 7 Apply the knowledge to resolve the issues** – By applying the knowledge, a greater understanding will be gained concerning the original issues. This will enable the group to identify skills needed to tackle the issues and to provide the necessary support from specialists if necessary.

- **Stage 8 Action plan** – Develop an action plan and a strategy to monitor effectiveness of change – this should be reviewed at regular intervals to ensure the needs of the learner with ADHD are being met.

The systemic analysis model (Cooper, 2006)

The systemic analysis model proposed by Cooper (2006) takes into account six factors that may have an impact on the child's functioning, as shown in Figure 3.2.

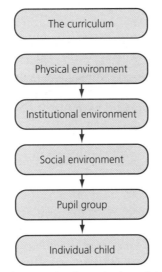

Fig 3.2: The systemic analysis (progressive focussing) model (Cooper, 2006, cited Hughes and Cooper, 2007, p65)

By considering each factor in isolation and reflecting on the impact each has on the behaviour of the child, the practitioner is able to form a clear picture of what triggers the child's behaviours. This provides a framework for the teacher to identify any similarities/differences in behaviour when it is influenced by different factors. The model also identifies whether an environment has an effect on behaviour, and this may assist the teacher in meeting the needs of the pupil with ADHD more effectively, as the teacher may be able to ensure that the trigger to the behaviour is minimised.

Strategies for working with children with ADHD in the classroom

When working with children who have ADHD keep in mind the following:

● Avoid behaviour problems by planning well and beginning instruction promptly. Offer directions as soon as the children enter the room, as transitional times are often the worst times for children with ADHD.

- Make directions clear and short. Use short sentences when explaining tasks. Repeat if necessary and split tasks into smaller steps in order that they do not appear too daunting to the child.
- Assist the child with organising their materials and workplace, and organisation of their time, by providing a clear structure and training the child to follow instructions.
- Offer positive reinforcement frequently in different forms. Children are motivated to work for tangible rewards such as stickers and prizes.
- Offer a creative approach, using interesting materials, hands-on activities, visual and auditory aids.
- Consider classroom environment, for example reduce clutter, as this will avoid further distraction for the child. Ensure noise is not excessive.
- Always have a back-up plan in case the child becomes bored/frustrated.
- Allow any child who has ADHD and who becomes restless to move around; failure to do this will result in more anxiety.
- Mix active and quiet periods. Allow the child extra time to make the transition from one task to another.
- Set aside an area in the classroom where the child may go when feeling out of control. This will allow the child time to calm down.
- Assist the child in developing his/her own strategies for when their behaviour gets out of control.

Differentiate the child from the behaviour: see the child first, then the behaviour.

Conclusion

The aim of teachers, practitioners and parents is to provide an inclusive environment for the pupil with ADHD and to develop coping strategies in order that the child may develop the necessary confidence to be an able member of society. Any child who has ADHD is reliant on the support of teachers, practitioners and parents to ensure that he/she is able to reach his/her maximum potential with regard to academic and social development. It is important to realise that changing the child's behaviour will only happen over time, and understanding the child with ADHD through collaborative work should be central in order to shape the child's environment via a consistent and cohesive approach.

Key ideas summary

- Think about what you have learnt about ADHD.

- What are the characteristics of ADHD?

- How do you identify ADHD?

- Is it possible to meet the needs of the pupil with ADHD in a mainstream environment?

- Does your school consider the factors identified in this chapter when working with the pupil with ADHD?

- Do staff use either of the models identified in this chapter to solve the problems faced by the pupil who has ADHD?

- What are the most important things to consider when in the classroom with a pupil with ADHD?

Going further

References and further reading

Anastopolous, A. (1999) 'ADHD', in Netherton, S., Holmes, C. and Walker, C. (eds) *Child and Adolescent Psychological Disorders: A Comprehensive Textbook*, Oxford: Oxford University Press.

APA (1994) (4th edn) *Diagnostic and Statistical Manual of Mental Disorders*, Washington, DC: APA.

Burrows, H.S. and Tamblyn, R.M. (1980) *Problem-based Learning: An Approach to Medical Education*, New York: Springer.

Cantwell, D. (1975) *The Hyperactive Child: Diagnosis Management and Current Research*, New York: Spectrum.

Hughes, L. and Cooper, P. (2007) *Understanding and Supporting Children with ADHD*, London: Sage.

Jones, C. (2004) *Supporting Inclusion in the Early Years*, Maidenhead: McGraw Hill. Special Educational Needs and Disability Act 2001, available from http://www.opsi.gov.uk/Acts, accessed June 2008.

Tannock, R. (1998) 'ADHD: Advances in cognitive neurobiological and genetic research', *Journal of Child Psychology and Psychiatry*, 39(1) 65–99.

Thompson, R. (1993) (2nd edn) *The Brain: A Neuroscience Primer*, New York: Freeman.

→

Times Education Supplement (2008) *How to spot ADHD*, available from http://www.tes.co.uk, accessed June 2008.

Wender, P. H. (2000) *ADHD: ADHD in children, adolescents and adults*, New York: Oxfordline Press.

Social, emotional and behavioural difficulties

What this chapter will explore:

- What are social, emotional and behavioural difficulties (SEBD)?
- What is appropriate behaviour?
- Theories of SEBD
- Identifying symptoms of SEBD
- Strategies to change behaviour
- Top tips for practitioners when reinforcing behaviours
- Working with others to support children with SEBD

This chapter is concerned with social, emotional and behavioural difficulties and the effect these have on the learning and development of young people. The chapter is intended to help you to identify a child with social, emotional and behavioural difficulties and adopt strategies you can introduce into your own classroom to help both you and the child work and learn together more effectively.

What are social, emotional and behavioural difficulties?

Social, emotional and behavioural difficulties (SEBD) can be a significant challenge for any practitioner; they often appear in the form of disruptive behaviour in the classroom and school environment. Behavioural difficulties may be demonstrated such that pupils will be prevented from learning and teaching may be practically impossible due to the disruptive behaviour of the individual. This may even result in physically aggressive behaviour to both teachers and other students. In contrast, emotional difficulties tend to be demonstrated by the individual student being very withdrawn.

When working with people with behavioural and emotional difficulties we need to remember that if there is a 'problem behaviour' it does not follow that there is a 'problem child' and there may be a number of reasons why the individual is displaying inappropriate behaviour. It may be that the individual has not developed social skills at the same level as his/her peers, or that the individual has low self-esteem and as a result is unable to form relationships with his/her peers. It may also be that the individual's needs are not being met; an example of this may be the child who lives in conflict at home and comes from a disadvantaged background. The child may suffer from malnutrition or abuse at home and as a result may demonstrate aggressive behaviour at school as a means of gaining attention.

It is important to distinguish that if a child does not understand the concept of the word 'naughty' due to his/her immature social skills the behaviour exhibited is likely to continue. On entering the school environment, a child may display behavioural problems due to his/her insecurity in the new environment, or as a result of a lack of confidence when being introduced to other new children. If we think of behaviour in this way what may at first seem inappropriate behaviour may actually be a coping strategy for the child who is placed in an unfamiliar educational environment.

For some children behavioural difficulties are very hard to overcome. We need to remember that their cognitive and social development may be affected, and as a result the children may have learning difficulties, which could lead to problems with accessing the curriculum. In contrast, learning difficulties may result in a child displaying behavioural difficulties as a result of being frustrated at being unable to access the curriculum in the educational environment.

What is appropriate behaviour?

When talking about inappropriate behaviour we should be clear what *appropriate* behaviour is, in order that as practitioners working with children we are able to identify inappropriate behaviour in children when it occurs. Mortimer (2002, p16) suggests that desirable behaviour involves:

● feeling motivated and confident enough to develop to an individual's best potential
● being able to make friends and gain affection
● being able to express feelings in appropriate ways
● being able to 'do' when asked politely
● being able to make a useful contribution to the group
● developing positive self-esteem.

As practitioners we must be role models for the child in order for them to display desirable behaviour, and, if necessary, we show the child how to understand the right and wrong way to behave. One example of this may be when the child is playing and becomes very rough. This may be appropriate at times but at other times inappropriate. Another example might be when a child is playing in the ball pool area and becomes rough – this behaviour is acceptable; however, if the child were sitting listening to a story then rough play is not appropriate. The role of the practitioner is to ensure that the child is aware of the boundaries and when rough play is acceptable and when it isn't.

By reinforcing positive behaviour and constantly using modelling techniques, applying language such as 'Please' and 'Thank you', a child is more likely to imitate this behaviour and it will become second nature after a while. Failure to use positive reinforcement may result in the child being disruptive, as constant negative reinforcement can reduce their self-esteem and confidence, and as a result the child may demonstrate emotional difficulties in the form of withdrawal from activities in the educational environment.

I will share an example of this from my own practice. When working recently with a child who had social, emotional and behavioural difficulties I always referred to this child by his first name and reinforced every task he completed by saying 'Thank you, Robert'. Even when he put his chair under the table at the end of the day I applied language such as 'Robert, how lovely to see you helping by putting your chair under the table.' Within a month Robert was imitating this behaviour with other children and when they helped each other or carried out a task Robert would say 'How lovely to see you helping.' The positive reinforcement constantly offered by myself obviously had an impact on Robert's behaviour.

Theories of SEBD

Research evidence

Theoretical explanations of SEBD include a model proposed by Patterson et al. (1992, cited in Hunter-Carsch, 2006, p2), who suggest that individuals become anti-social as a result of specific factors including:

- social disadvantage
- ineffective parental discipline
- lack of parental supervision
- parental use of physical punishment
- parental rejection
- peer rejection
- membership of deviant peer group
- academic failure
- low self-esteem.

It is suggested by Patterson et al. that family and school factors can interact in negative ways in order to make worse the symptoms of SEBD. They describe a four-stage process:

Stage 1   Pre-school phase – Child is trained in inappropriate behaviour at home by parents and family members, who act as models reinforcing the negative behaviours.

Stage 2   The social environment reacts – When child enters school, behaviours that were appropriate at home are challenged, and child's behaviour escalates even further, which leads to the child being in conflict both at home and at school.

Stage 3   Deviant peers and polishing anti-social skills – Due to the rejection at home and school, child seeks out other like-minded children who then form a deviant group. Skills of coercion reinforced and developed.

Stage 4   The career anti-social adult – The resultant adult may be socially excluded, as his/her way of relating to others is through coercion, and as a result it may be difficult for him/her to form personal relationships.

Psychological factors

Maslow (cited in Woolfolk, Hughes and Walkup, 2008) proposed a hierarchy of needs, whereby if a child's needs are not met he/she is more likely to demonstrate symptoms of SEBD. For example, if a child is not given breakfast prior to attending school, he/she may display aggressive behaviour on entering school merely due to the fact that he/she is hungry and his/her needs are not being met.

Maslow's hierarchy of needs include:

- self-actualisation
- self-esteem
- affiliation
- safety
- physiological.

If an individual is unable to get his/her safety needs met this may result in that individual experiencing feelings of insecurity and as a result being unable to relate to other people in appropriate ways. As a result the individual is unable to form affiliations with others and specific needs therefore are not met. (See Figure 4.1).

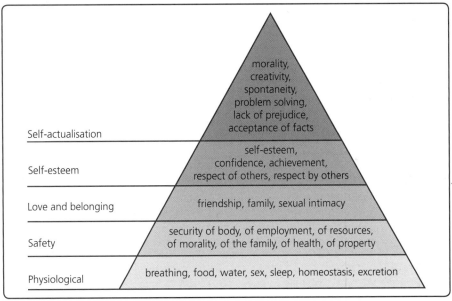

Fig 4.1: Maslow's hierarchy of needs
Source: Based on Maslow, A.H. (1943), 'A theory of human motivation', *Psychological Review*, 50 (4) 370–96. This content is in the public domain.

Biopsychosocial factors

Uta Frith (1992, cited in Hunter-Carsch et al., 2006, p6) proposed a model of the relationship between biological causes and behavioural difficulties. This model demonstrates that experience, maturation, motivation and compensation act as mediators between biological characteristics and actual behaviour (see Figure 4.2 overleaf).

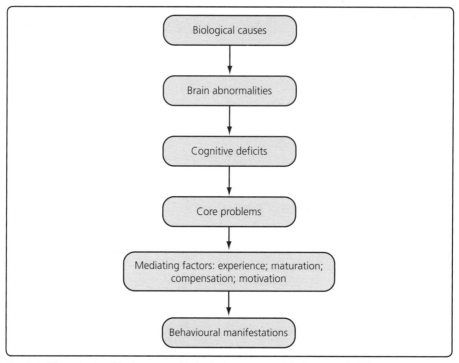

Fig 4.2: The relationship between biological causes and behavioural difficulties (Adapted from Frith, 1992, cited in Hunter-Carsch, 2006, p7)

Frith's model suggests that biological factors are not alone in determining the behaviour of the individual. Factors including social environment, interpersonal relationships, educational interventions and individual's attitudes, beliefs and attributions also influence the behaviour somewhat.

Culture and society

Hunter-Carsch et al. (2006) suggest that these models only offer *some* explanation of the causes or roots of SEBD. They argue that the causes of SEBD are due to social and cultural factors. An increase in these problems is apparent by observing that between 1992 and 1998 the annual number of exclusions from school in England rose, and four times as many pupils were excluded in the latter year.

Identifying symptoms of SEBD

If you are working with a child in your educational setting and you have cause for concern with regard to his/her behaviour, ask yourself the following questions

TOP TIP!

If you suspect that a child has social, emotional or behavioural difficulties it may be a good idea to note down each time the behaviour occurs, how often it occurs and what the circumstances are. This will enable you to form a clear picture of the child and identify whether the child needs referral to a specialist in order for diagnosis to take place.

to help you decide whether there is a need for an intervention programme. The questions are based on Somerset County Council (2009).

- Does the child find it difficult to follow instructions?
- Does the child have poor concentration?
- Is the child unable to finish tasks without additional support?
- Does the child find it difficult to play alongside others?
- Does the child find it difficult to share with others and find an awareness of the needs of others difficult?
- Does the child demand attention and become disruptive if kept waiting?

If the answers to the above questions are yes, consider whether the child has actually had time to adjust to his/her new surroundings, as this may be the cause of the inappropriate behaviour. It may be useful to communicate with parents/carers as they will be able to offer vital information that may confirm your concerns with regard to the issues being faced by the child. If in contrast the child has been in the educational environment for some time and his/her behaviour has become disruptive or has not changed following an adjustment period, it may be that the child needs extra support in order to overcome his/her barriers to learning caused by the disruptive behaviour.

Strategies to change behaviour

When working with a child who has behavioural difficulties it is important to identify opportunities to change the behaviour whenever possible. This may involve using some of the following strategies:

- Employing a teaching assistant to work with the child when reading a book on a one-to-one basis in order that the child does not become disruptive when he/she is unable to sit still and listen alongside his/her peers.

- Distracting the child from the disruptive behaviour. An example of this may be when the child is ripping paper rather than writing on it, distract the child and engage him/her in writing by being a role model and offering positive reinforcement 'Let's write together. I know you are very good at writing.'

- Set achievable tasks at the correct level as failure to do this may result in the child displaying disruptive behaviour as a means of distraction from a task that he/she finds too difficult to complete. By setting achievable targets, and tasks, the self-esteem and confidence of the child will be raised and as a result the disruptive behaviour may decrease.

- Remember to use positive reinforcement for any good behaviour, and for any task completed, no matter how small, as this will also raise the self-esteem of the child.

- Offer clear instructions to the child who has SEBD, and ensure that they have understood what is expected of them; for example, if they are to complete a task within a specific time frame make this clear. Failure to do so may result in the child presenting difficult behaviours as he/she does not fully understand what is expected of him/her and as a result will become very frustrated and have feelings of insecurity.

- Model behaviour, as it may not be enough to offer verbal instructions to the child. It may be necessary to show the child what to do.

Top tips for practitioners when reinforcing behaviours

When setting tasks consider the following (adapted from Fox, 2001, p40):

- Is the task set at the correct level?
- Is the individual able to work independently or does he/she require some extra help to complete the task?
- Does the individual have the necessary equipment to hand?
- Are the instructions clear?
- Is positive reinforcement offered on a regular basis?
- Is there frequent checking of the task?
- Is positive feedback offered?

UsefulWebsite

http://www.teachingexpertise.com/articles/emotional-and-behavioural-difficulties-ebd-1226

This website is excellent as it provides strategies to support individuals with emotional and behavioural difficulties. There are also links to practical tips that can be used for behaviour management in the classroom.

Research evidence

Mortimer (2002, p21) suggests the ABC approach to behaviour management. This approach is based on the theory of behavioural psychology and is heavily dependent on the use of positive reinforcement and rewards. Mortimer suggests:

- If we do something, and something pleasant happens to us, we are more likely to do that thing again.

- If we do something and something unpleasant happens to us, we are less likely to do that thing again.

- The pleasant event is called a 'reward' simply because it makes the behaviour increase.

- The unpleasant event is called a 'punishment' simply because it makes the behaviour decrease.

- Punishment need not be something unpleasant that happens, it can simply be that the child was expecting a specific reward and this did not ensue.

Reflecting on practice

Jasbinder has been displaying social and emotional behavioural difficulties since she started school at the age of four. She was disruptive in class, especially during literacy hour. Her behaviour included physical violence in the form of pinching her peers and kicking staff, and she also shouts verbal abuse at her peers and staff when she is asked to complete literacy tasks. Jasbinder's parents had not noticed the behaviour prior to her starting school, although they had noticed that when they tried to engage her with any books she became disruptive.

→

Consider the following:

1. Have you come across children with similar behavioural problems to Jasbinder in your class?
2. How have you reacted to this child?
3. What positive behaviour support strategies can you use that might result in an improvement in Jasbinder's behaviour?

Working with others to support children with SEBD

In order to ensure an inclusive approach for children with SEBD in an educational setting it is imperative that individual practitioners take a holistic approach. This includes:

- Supporting each other in the educational environment, to ensure a consistent approach is taken. As discussed in Chapter 2, the SENCO has a key role to ensure that staff are offered support and guidance when working with pupils with SEBD.
- Involving children with SEBD and their parents in the development of whole-school policies, by communicating with parents and inviting them into the school to be involved in the decision-making process with regard to the child's education.
- Ensuring that practitioners are suitably trained to work with children who have SEBD. Such training may be offered by the behaviour support team through the local authority.
- Provide supportive environments to promote all children's development. An example of this is where a child is offered the opportunity to attend a nurture group, which will enable the child to gain confidence working alongside a very small number of pupils rather than in a classroom environment with up to 30 children.

Conclusion

The aim of teachers, practitioners and parents is to provide an inclusive environment for the child with SEBD and to develop coping strategies in order to meet the individual needs of the child. In order to ensure this occurs, early identification and support is essential to maximise the learning opportunities of the individual child. Practitioners are well placed to identify children who may display characteristics of SEBD; however, it is imperative that practitioners have the necessary training to be effective in meeting their needs.

Key ideas summary

- Think about what you have learned about social, emotional and behavioural difficulties.

- What are SEBD?

- How do you identify SEBD?

- What strategies can you use in order to meet the needs of the individual with SEBD?

- As a practitioner, how can you ensure an inclusive approach when working with individuals with SEBD?

Going further

References and further reading

Farrell, M. (2006) *The Effective Teacher's Guide to Behavioural, Emotional and Social Difficulties: Practical Strategies*, London: Routledge.

Fox, G. (2001) *Supporting Children with Behaviour Difficulties: A Guide for Assistants in Schools*, London: David Fulton.

Hunter-Carsch, M., Tiknaz, Y., Cooper, P. and Sage, R. (2006) *The Handbook of Social, Emotional and Behavioural Difficulties*, London: Continuum.

Mortimer, H. (2002) *Behavioural and Emotional Difficulties*, Leamington Spa: Scholastic.

Somerset County Council (2009) *Early Identification of Social, Emotional and Behavioural Difficulties,* http://www.six.somerset.gov.uk/sixv3/do_download.asp?did=15395, accessed February 2009.

Woolfolk, A., Hughes, M. and Walkup, V. (2008) *Psychology in Education*, Harlow: Pearson Education.

Dyslexia

What this chapter will explore:

- Theories of dyslexia
- Key characteristics of dyslexia
- Identifying and assessing dyslexia in the classroom
- Classroom management
- Top tips for teachers
- Planning for learning

This chapter will offer an overview of the different theories of dyslexia. It is intended to help you identify children who may display characteristics of dyslexia, and to assist you in providing an effective educational working environment for these children. Classroom management strategies will be offered and some useful hints and tips provided to assist you and the child to work and learn together more effectively. Support and guidance will be offered to educators to develop an understanding of the complexities of dyslexia. Early identification and a clear understanding of the characteristics of dyslexia are imperative in order that the teacher feels more confident and skilled to deal with students with dyslexia in the educational environment.

Theories of dyslexia

It is not surprising that the subject of dyslexia as a disability is controversial, as the sheer nature of acquiring literacy skill is very complex. There may be many reasons why individuals find it difficult to learn to read, write or spell; however, these individuals are not all considered 'dyslexic'. While the child who does not have dyslexia develops language 'as they build on other cognitive abilities by actively trying to make sense of what they hear and by looking for patterns and making up rules to put together the jigsaw puzzle of language' (Brookes, 1997, Woolfolk et al., 2008, p64), this is clearly not the case for the child with dyslexia. There is much debate about the causes of dyslexia. Most authors agree that the areas of the brain associated with language processing are involved (Brookes, 1997, cited in Woolfolk et al., 2008, p65). This is indicative that the language acquisition of a child with dyslexia is very different to that of a child without the condition.

The term dyslexic has been used as it was coined from the Greek and literally means difficulty with (dys) words (lexis) (Pollock et al., 2004). Prior to the term dyslexia being used, 'individuals had been seen to experience diminution or loss of the ability to read, write or speak following strokes or blows to the head' (Pollak, 2005, p1). Dating back as far as 1925 dyslexia was viewed as a visual issue, and early researchers suggested that difficulties may be hereditary, and involve difficulties with speech, spelling and reading, leading to labelling as a dunce in the classroom (Pollak, 2005). Similarly, Miles (1993) reinforces the work of early pioneers, suggesting that dyslexia consists of a variety of disabilities rather than a single condition.

In contrast, the British Dyslexia Association defines dyslexia as a 'specific learning difficulty which mainly affects the development of literacy and language related skills' (British Dyslexia Association, 2008). This definition is quite clearly very broad and has received criticism as it focuses on learning to read and emphasises deficits, rather than applying the context with regard to the way in which literacy skills are acquired (Mortimore and Crozier, 2006, p235).

Theorists agree dyslexia is a condition whereby as a result of brain differences, the cognitive processes of individuals with dyslexia lead them to process information that is received from the brain differently. As a result some individuals who have dyslexia may experience difficulties with processing information. This difference may result in the individual struggling with tasks such as reading and writing, which may result in a disability in this area (DfES, 2004).

In contrast, the social interactive theory of dyslexia focuses on how society reacts to dyslexia, specifically by concentrating on social values. This theory views learning differences as a reflection of deficits in the learner and argues that as a result of social perceptions and values, the individual's disability arises (DfES, 2004, p34). The biological theory of dyslexia suggests that brain deficiency is the reason for cognitive difficulties in the individual with dyslexia. Another view of dyslexia is that phonological processing difficulties are predominant in individuals who have dyslexia to greater or lesser degrees (DfES, 2004, p35). This statement offered by the DfES is vague and questionable as there is no reference to further research to reinforce these findings.

Elliott (2005, p728) argues against the 'common understanding of dyslexia as a myth which hides the scandal of true reading disability.' The British Psychological Society (1999, cited in Elliott, 2005, p728) suggests:

> *Dyslexia is evident when accurate and fluent word reading and/or spelling develops very incompletely or with very great difficulty. This focuses on literacy learning at the 'word' level and implies that the problem is severe and persistent despite appropriate learning opportunities.*

With this in mind, it is questionable whether the existence of dyslexia is a myth. Nicolson (2005, cited in Elliott, 2005) points out that dyslexia cannot be a myth, as 50 per cent of the variance in dyslexia is genetic and as such this condition is clear and distinct. Nicolson further comments: 'No one has ever suggested that children with generalised learning difficulties can't learn to read', further highlighting that although dyslexia may demonstrate a deficit in literacy learning, it does not result in the child being completely helpless and unable to learn.

It is evident that debates continue in relation to the extent of the nature of learning difficulties involved, their diagnosis and the form that any interventions should take (Mortimer and Crozier, 2006, p235). However, guidelines have been published concerning students with dyslexia which are indicative of the problems that may be encountered with regard to study skills. These include memorising names and facts, remembering sequences, problems with time keeping, concentration, writing, copying and word retrieval (Klein, 1993, cited in Mortimer and Crozier, 2006, p237).

UsefulWebsite

http://www.excellencegateway.org.uk/page.aspx?o=126809

This website will offer you more information about the theories of dyslexia. There are also links to the different theories, and case studies.

Key characteristics of dyslexia

There are many theoretical explanations of the key characteristics of dyslexia, the most common being that a pupil with dyslexia may have problems with phonological development, visual processing, working memory and information-processing speed.

Reflecting on practice

Sarah, a six-year-old girl, has recently moved primary schools and has found it very difficult settling into her new school. She always complains that there is not enough time to copy from the board and says she loses her place. Sarah is becoming very frustrated as although she is trying really hard, she cannot find her place, the words are very jumbled up and it takes her a long time to check her work. When the teacher checks Sarah's work there are lots of mistakes. Sarah also finds it very difficult to write and doesn't always understand what she has written. She has started to become isolated from her peers as she lacks confidence when writing in class.

This highlights the issues that a child who may have dyslexia may face in the classroom. It is clear from Sarah's story that she is struggling to cope without literacy support in the classroom.

Consider the following:

1. Is there a child in your class who demonstrates characteristics like Sarah's?

2. What strategies are put in place to support the child with his/her learning?

3. If you have established that a child has dyslexia, how would you adapt the working environment for this child?

In your career you will no doubt come across a child who displays some characteristics that may identify them as having dyslexia. To assist you with identifying the child as having the condition, Dyslexia UK (2009) identifies the following characteristics that may be present in children with dyslexia.

Behaviour

- Daydreams or drifts off into own private world
  - forgets easily, particularly recent things but may have a good memory for things that happened a long time ago

- Finds it difficult to deal with more than one instruction at a time
- Extremes in mood, lack of calm 'middle ground'
  - little sense of time
- Can be very stubborn
- Can be quiet, withdrawn and anxious
- Doesn't like change
- Has tantrums
- Easily distracted
- Intolerant of noise
- Appears not to listen
- May have speech problems
- May lack coordination and spill things or knock things over
- May have allergies
- May have stress-related illnesses
- A child might seem to be completely different when attending school to how they were pre-school.

Reading

- Cannot master reading at all or mastered it very late
- Can read to self but 'out loud' makes lots of mistakes
- Can read stories but has problems with exam questions and anything technical
- Can read perfectly but doesn't get much meaning from what has been read
- Needs to re-read to make sense
  - skips lines
- Loses place
- Dislikes reading and tries to avoid it
  - starts OK but gets progressively worse
- Reverses syllables or words
- Leaves out, misreads or substitutes small words such as 'was' and 'they'
- Can read a word on one page and misread the same word on another.

Handwriting

- Handwriting may be illegible
- Handwriting legible only if very slow
  - heavy pressure on page (presses very hard with pen or pencil)
- Difficulties joining letters
- Strange spacing
- Letters formed strangely to disguise spelling problems
- Writing process highly stressful and very tiring.

Spelling

- Words spelt as they sound
- Bizarre spelling producing unrecognisable words
- Letters repeated: 'rememember' for 'remember'
- Letters left out 'rember' for 'remember'
- Letters reversed 'brid' for 'bird'
- Mistakes made with small words such as 'thay' for 'they'
- Spellings rote learnt for tests but can't then apply them in writing.

Writing composition

- Writing disorganised and writer gets lost in the process
- Difficulties starting
- Sentences muddled
- Content pictured as a whole but unable to get it down sequentially
- Thoughts too fast for pen
- Small words missed or used wrongly
- Frequent crossings out
- Writer can't see mistakes
- Finds writing is immensely frustrating and avoids where possible
- Finds writing is a slow process and may involve many drafts if despair doesn't set in first.

Punctuation

- Punctuation is not used at all
- Some punctuation is used but is not understood
- Writer has no sense of where the marks should go, even though they have been told.

Maths

- May be excellent at maths
- May find all of maths difficult
- Cannot grasp what is required from the maths question
- Loses track when following procedures, e.g. long multiplication
- Directional difficulties, e.g. instead of going from right to left with addition, subtraction and multiplication, will work the other way
- Gets muddled between maths symbols
- Difficulties learning times tables
  - problems with place value (hundreds, tens and units)
- Reverses numbers
- Makes many small mistakes
- Finds mental maths difficult because the sum 'goes' before the calculation is complete
- Can get the answers but can't show the workings out.

Talents

- Often have excellent 'people skills'
- Can be good at problem solving
- Can think three dimensionally, giving rise to talents in such areas as design, computing, acting
- Can be very good at sport
- Can be good at art, particularly 3D
- Often highly intuitive
- Very curious about how things work
- Highly aware of their environment and often notice details
- Thinks in an original way

- Thinks holistically
- Often very good at Lego as a child.

Any of these characteristics may be present, although it is important to realise that the learning context may have a tremendous impact on how the individual with dyslexia progresses in education. If the learning environment is dyslexia-friendly this helps to reduce the impact of dyslexia on the individual (Reid, 2007, pxi). If the practitioner does not take into account the individual needs of the learner who has dyslexia, this will cause much anxiety and as a result the child's education may be affected. The British Dyslexia Association's website contains lots of further information about dyslexia including advice for individuals with dyslexia, parents, and how to apply for an assessment to identify dyslexia (http://www.bdadyslexia.org.uk).

Reflecting on practice

Kyra, a six-year-old primary school pupil, is finding it increasingly difficult to distinguish the letter 'b' from the letter 'd' when asked to write in class. Kyra also has difficulty in visualising the difference between words such as 'was' and 'saw'. This has lead to Kyra becoming very quiet and withdrawn, and when she is asked to complete any written work it is noticeable that she becomes very anxious. Other children in the class have started to notice that Kyra finds reading difficult and are making fun of her, exacerbating the problems even further.

Consider the following:

1. Have you come across children with similar difficulties with literacy?
2. How have you supported this child?
3. How could you adapt the learning environment to meet the needs of this child?

Identifying and assessing dyslexia in the classroom

It is important that children with dyslexia are identified early in order that opportunities are available to ensure they are able to progress in education. Teachers in primary school are well placed to identify any difficulties a child may be having with literacy that may need investigating to ensure the child does not have dyslexia. In secondary schools, the English teacher would also be well placed to identify any literacy difficulties that may be demonstrated. By carrying out observations a practitioner would be able to gather specific evidence relating to issues with reading, writing or spelling prior to consulting the SENCO for advice and guidance.

The *SEN Code* (DfES, 2001) suggests that 'children who demonstrate ... specific learning difficulties such as dyslexia ... require specific programmes to aid progress in cognition and learning. Some of these children may have associated sensory, physical and behavioural difficulties that compound their needs' (7:58). As stated in Chapter 2, triggers for School Action may be the teacher or other individuals who work closely with the child who may have concerns about their reading, writing and spelling, along with evidence to show that they are having difficulties with literacy. If, following intervention, the child receives additional or differentiated learning opportunities to target the specific weaknesses and little or no progress is made; this stage of the intervention is termed School Action. At this point, the SENCO and teacher will produce an action plan to assist the child with progression. Specialist equipment may be offered to meet the child's individual needs and some individual support may be required.

School Action Plus may be deemed necessary if, despite receiving an individualised programme and extra support, the child still has difficulties. At this stage a decision is taken in collaboration with parents as to whether to bring in outside specialists to measure the child's progress with a view to ensuring that the necessary support is available to enable the child to continue progressing in a mainstream environment.

Interestingly Gavin Reid, an experienced writer focusing on dyslexia, suggests:

> *Dyslexia should not only be identified through the use of a test: assessment for dyslexia is a process that considers the classroom and curriculum factors and the learning preferences of the child, as well as his or her specific learning difficulties.*

(Reid, 2007, p22)

Thus it is important that assessment for dyslexia involves much more than a test. Reid (2007, pp 22–3) advocates that assessment should consider three aspects, as follows.

Difficulties

It is clear that children with dyslexia tend to have problems with encoding and decoding print. These difficulties may be as a result of difficulties in:

- acquiring phonological awareness
- memory
- organisation and sequencing
- movement and coordination
- language problems
- visual/auditory perception.

Discrepancies

Discrepancies may prevail when children are reading/listening with regard to decoding information, between oral and written skills, and when working across the curriculum in different subject areas.

Differences

We need to remember that not every child with dyslexia will have the same difficulties, and with this in mind the identification process should consider the following:

● learning styles
● environmental preferences for learning
● learning strategies.

Research evidence

A number of different assessments may be carried out to determine whether a child has dyslexia. Goodman (1969, cited in DCSF, 2009) first introduced the term 'miscue analysis', which was based on three 'cueing' systems:

● grapho/phonic – the relationship of letters to sound system
● syntactic – the syntax/grammar system
● semantic – the meaning system

The miscues were able to identify both the readers' strengths and weaknesses, but would enable the practitioner to identify what the learner understands about the text. Connect and extend for further information to http://www.dcsf.gov.uk/readwriteplus/bank/Miscue%20Analysis.pdf

Top tips for identifying dyslexia

There is not a specific checklist for identifying dyslexia. However, in order to gain a preliminary insight into the strengths and weaknesses of a child Reid (2007) offers the following suggestions.

Although these checklists can form the basis of a preliminary assessment in relation to the difficulties a child may be facing with reading and writing, the teacher should carry out further, more in-depth assessments with regard to any specific difficulties in order that the child can be identified having dyslexia. Many of the characteristics of dyslexia may be obvious in the classroom environment; however, teachers must have a clear understanding of dyslexia in order to be able to identify a child who has this learning difficulty.

Reading	Comments
Sight vocabulary	
Sound blending	
Use of contextual clues	
Attempting unknown vocabulary	
Eye tracking	
Difficulty keeping place	
Speech development	
Motivation in relation to reading material	
Word-naming difficulty	
Omitting words	
Omitting phrases	
Omitting whole lines	

Writing	Comments
Directional difficulty	
Difficulty associating visual symbol with verbal sound	
Liable to sub-vocalise sounds before writing	
Unusual spelling pattern	
Handwriting difficulty	
Difficulty with cursive writing	
Using capitals and lower case interchangeably and inconsistently	
Poor organisation of work on page	

TOP TIP!

If you suspect that a child has dyslexia it may be a good idea to use the above checklist to note down the details of any difficulties he/she may face. This will enable you to form a general picture of the child and identify whether referral to a specialist for diagnosis is necessary.

Classroom management

All schools will have some children with dyslexia, and an awareness of specific teaching methods and practical approaches for those children is vital for class teachers. From

UsefulWebsite

Visit http://www.dyslexiaaction.org.uk/

This website is useful if you wish to find out more about identifying and assessing children for dyslexia.

my experience of working with children who have dyslexia, the following suggestions may be useful in order to move towards an inclusive and effective classroom:

- When offering instructions to a child with dyslexia, only give one instruction at a time to enable the child to process the information effectively.
  - Make use of information technology by using voice recognition software.
  - Ensure that the child who has dyslexia is given extra time to complete reading/writing tasks if required.
  - Use visual and kinaesthetic teaching approaches to facilitate the learning for the child.
  - Communicate with the SENCO and teaching assistants on a regular basis to ensure that a consistent approach is offered to the child with dyslexia.
  - Avoid distractions in the classroom as the student with dyslexia may find it hard to concentrate in class.

Why not try this?

Practise planning for a student who has dyslexia by taking a single lesson objective and developing different activities that may suit a visual and kinaesthetic learner.

Top tips for teachers

From my experience of working with children who have dyslexia it is clear that along with having difficulty remembering more than one instruction at a time, they may find it hard to hold more than one point in their memory. With this in mind, when teaching a child with dyslexia we need to remember the following:

- When planning tasks break these down into sizeable chunks to help organise the learning.

- Ensure that the tasks are clearly structured and sequenced to aid the organisation of the learning.
- Provide a checklist at the start and end of each task to ensure the child with dyslexia is aware of the expectations.

Planning for learning

The following checklist will be useful when planning worksheets:

- Is the font big enough?
- Are there too many words on the page?
- Are visuals used wherever possible?
- Are all sentences supported with visual representations?

Reading and making meaning

When trying to engage a child who has dyslexia with reading it is useful to encourage the children to ask themselves the following questions after the reading session:

- What can I remember about this book?
- What is my favourite part of the book?
- Who were the main characters?
- What ideas were important in the book?
- What questions do I want to ask about the book?

These reading strategies are likely to encourage the child who has dyslexia to engage with the story and may help him/her to read for meaning rather than merely reading the words.

Reflecting on practice

James, a child with dyslexia, finds it difficult to copy work from the white-board. James complains during each session that he does not have time to copy all the information on the board and he loses his place. He gets very frustrated as he makes lots of mistakes, and when his teacher checks his work he always has to stay behind to finish copying from the board. James finds it difficult to read the writing and the words seem to move around and get very confused. →

Consider the following:

1. Have you come across children with similar difficulties to James in your class?
2. What strategies have you put in place to ensure effective learning?
3. How do you feel you could adapt the learning environment to meet the needs of this child?
4. What materials can you produce that may help the child to learn more effectively?

Some ideas from Reid (2007, p95) are:

- Provide the child with a copy of the work on the whiteboard and ask him/her to highlight the key points in the work.
- Offer Text Help to assist with spellchecking. This offers a read-back facility.
- Make a list of words that the child with dyslexia usually misspells and ask him/her to put the meaning of the word next to it.

Conclusion

As teachers and practitioners, the ultimate aim is to ensure that the child with dyslexia is not disadvantaged in the learning environment in comparison to his/her peers as a result of the disability. In order to raise the self-esteem and confidence of children who have dyslexia it is crucial that a range of teaching procedures for literacy are considered. It should also be appreciated that every child with dyslexia is unique and, while one approach may work for one child, it should not be a 'one size fits all' approach, and different teaching approaches may be required for each child.

Key ideas summary

- Think about what you have learnt about dyslexia.
- What are the characteristics of dyslexia?
- How do you identify and assess dyslexia?
- How do teachers determine if a child is dyslexic in your class?
- Does the teacher use a checklist to record any difficulties which may be apparent with literacy?
- What strategies are put into place to enable the dyslexic child to progress with reading and writing?
- What are the most important things to consider when in the classroom with the dyslexic pupil?

Going further

References and further reading

British Dyslexia Association (2008) *Definition of Dyslexia*, www.bdadyslexia. org.uk, accessed June 2009.

DCSF (2009) *Miscue Analysis*, http://rwp.excellencegateway.org.uk/ readwriteplus/bank/Miscue%20Analysis.pdf, accessed January 2010.

DfES (2001) *The Special Educational Needs Code of Practice*, Nottingham: DfES, http://www.teachernet.gov.uk/_doc/3724/SENCodeOfPractice.pdf.

DfES (2004) *A Framework for Understanding Dyslexia*, Leicester: NIACE.

Dyslexia UK (2009) *Some Common Dyslexia Characteristics in Children*, http://www.dyslexia-uk.org/ChildCharact.html, accessed June 2009.

Elliott, J. (2005) 'The dyslexia debate continues' *The Psychologist*, 18 (12), 728–30, http://www.thepsychologist.org.uk/archive/archive_home.cfm? volumeID=18&editionID=130&ArticleID=959, accessed November 2008.

Farrell, M. (2006) *The Effective Teacher's Guide to Dyslexia and other Specific Learning Difficulties*, Abingdon: Routledge.

Hartras, D. (2006) *Dyslexia in the Early Years: A Practical Guide to Teaching and Learning*, Abingdon: Routledge.

Miles, T. (1993) *Dyslexia: The Pattern of Difficulties*, London: Whurr.

Mortimore, T. and Crozier, R. (2006) 'Dyslexia and difficulties with study skills in higher education', *Studies in Higher Education*, 31(2) 235–251.

Pollak, D. (2005) *Dyslexia, The Self and Higher Education,* Stoke-on-Trent: Trentham.

Pollock, J., Waller, E. and Politt, R. (2004) (2nd edn) *Day-to-Day Dyslexia in the Classroom*, London: RoutledgeFalmer.

Reid, G. (2007) (2nd edn) *Dyslexia*, London: Continuum.

Riddick, B. (1995) 'Dyslexia: dispelling the myths', *Disability & Society*, 10(4), 457–73.

Thomson, M. (2003) *Dyslexia Included: A Whole School Approach*, London: David Fulton.

Woolfolk, A., Hughes, M. and Walkup, V. (2008) *Psychology in Education*, London: Pearson.

Websites

The British Dyslexia Association

www.bda-dyslexia.org.uk

Dyslexia Teacher

www.dyslexia-teacher.com

The Dyslexia Institute

www.dyslexia-inst.org.uk

www.dyslexiaassociation.ca

www.das.org.sg

Chapter

6

Dyspraxia

What this chapter will explore:

- What is dyspraxia?
- Key characteristics of dyspraxia
- Identifying dyspraxia in the classroom
- Top tips for identifying dyspraxia in the classroom
- Top tips for teachers/practitioners
- The learning environment

This chapter will offer educators an insight into dyspraxia, demonstrating the key characteristics of this complex special educational need. From my experience of working with children who have dyspraxia, they may demonstrate difficulties with everyday tasks such as getting dressed, running or handwriting. This chapter offers guidelines that may assist with the identification of dyspraxia and this will offer support to educators when working with a child who has dyspraxia. Hints and tips for ensuring an inclusive and effective educational environment will also be given throughout the chapter.

What is dyspraxia?

The name dyspraxia offers a description in itself, as 'dys' means 'faulty' and 'praxis' means 'the ability to use the body as a skilled tool' (Macintyre, 2001, p2). It is thought that dyspraxia affects up to 10 per cent of the population; males are more likely to be affected than females; and it is suggested that dyspraxia sometimes runs in families (Dyspraxic Foundation, 2009). Children who have no clear neurological disease, but may have difficulties in learning skills including eating with a spoon, speaking clearly, doing up buttons or riding a bike may be considered to have dyspraxia. From experience it is paramount that we reinforce that all children are unique and thus may display characteristics of dyspraxia which may be mild or severe, depending on their state of health and the environment they are in.

Children who have dyspraxia do have not have a general low level of attainment. They are able to understand what is wrong with them and, because of this, are able to develop coping strategies. A child with dyspraxia tends to develop skills such as walking, running, writing and talking later than their peers, but with support they are able to master these skills. Difficulties with language, perception and thought may be apparent. Children with dyspraxia look the same as other children, and this in itself may present a problem as a child's condition may not be recognised. It is therefore important that anyone working with a child who has dyspraxia recognises the cause of the difficulties and offers support to ensure that their specific needs are met.

Research evidence

The idea of dyspraxia has been discussed in the literature for the past 100 years, but there continues to be a lack of agreement regarding the definition of this disorder. The Dyspraxia Foundation (2009) suggest that developmental dyspraxia is

> 'An impairment or immaturity of the organisation of movement. It is an immaturity in the way that the brain processes information, which results in messages not being properly or fully transmitted. Dyspraxia affects the planning of what to do and how to do it. It is associated with problems of perception, language and thought.'

In contrast, researcher Dawdy (1981, cited in Ripley et al., 1997, p1) describes dyspraxia as 'impaired performance of skilled movements despite abilities within the average range and no significant findings on standard neurological examination'. Other researchers identify links with 'learning, language, visual perception and behavioural problems.' (Henderson and Sugden, 1992, cited in Ripley et al., 1997, p1).

UsefulWebsite

http://www.dyspraxiafoundation.org.uk/

This is a useful website for exploring dyspraxia in both children and adults. It also offers information on dyspraxia in education.

Key characteristics of dyspraxia

There are many characteristics that a child with dyspraxia may display, and from my experience of working with these children each one may display different characteristics, such as:

- clumsiness and a problem with coordination;
- overbalancing when changing direction;
- may have no sense of danger and therefore will need careful supervision when on playground equipment;
- may change hands halfway through an activity and seem confused about which hand to use;
- may find using pencils, scissors and simple toys hard;
- may have difficulty adapting to the structure and routines of school;
- may have poor concentration skills;
- may have poor listening skills;
- may display aggressive behaviour due to lack of coordination and the inability to control movements;
- may find it difficult to make friends due to poor social interaction skills.

Problems with movement

Recently, when working in a secondary special educational needs school, I noticed a child in the playground who displayed some characteristics that may have been linked to dyspraxia. She was wandering around very clumsily, but appeared to have no desire to become involved with any activities. It was interesting to note that this child found it very difficult to respond to instructions from her peers and as such she isolated herself from them to avoid being ridiculed. As a child with dyspraxia may have difficulties with coordination, activities that may be easy to other children, including hopscotch and playing with a ball, may cause that child great anxiety.

Coordination difficulties

Some children who display the symptoms of dyspraxia may have difficulties with whole body coordination, which can affect gross motor skills including running, jumping and climbing. In order to overcome these difficulties the child will have to remain very focused and concentrate on each step taken in order to prevent them from falling. In comparison a child without dyspraxia would not give this action a second thought. These difficulties may result in a child becoming withdrawn if asked to take part in sporting activities. A child, therefore, may need a great amount of positive reinforcement to gain the confidence to take part in such activities. In my experience of working with a child who has dyspraxia it is always a good idea to give the child a position of responsibility in order to raise his/her self-esteem. An example of this may be that, during sporting activities, you ask the child to be ball monitor, to give out the balls and collect them in. This will help a child feel much more involved and gain a sense of achievement and belonging to the group.

Fine motor skills may also prove to be a problem for a child with the symptoms of dyspraxia, and difficulties may be present when they carry out tasks such as writing and drawing. Strategies to overcome these problems will be discussed later in the chapter.

Problems with planning and organising

It is evident that some children with dyspraxia find it very difficult to plan, for example when playing ball during sports a child will be thinking 'I will have to move across the field to catch the ball.' In this instance the child may be unable to build a mental model of action and sequence the actions required to catch the ball. It is crucial to remain patient with a child when these difficulties occur and offer the child further time to carry out activities, as failure to do this will result in the child becoming very frustrated and anxious.

The Dyspraxia Foundation (2009) suggests that the following symptoms may be apparent at different stages of a young person's development.

The symptoms

By 3 years old

- Symptoms are evident from an early age. Babies are usually irritable from birth and may exhibit significant feeding problems.
- They are slow to achieve expected developmental milestones.
  For example, by the age of eight months they still may not sit independently.

- Many children with dyspraxia fail to go through the crawling stages, preferring to 'bottom shuffle' and then walk. They usually avoid tasks that require good manual dexterity.

Pre-school children – 3 to 5 year olds

- very high levels of motor activity, including feet swinging and tapping when seated, hand clapping or twisting; unable to stay still;
- high levels of excitability, with a loud/shrill voice;
- may be easily distressed and prone to temper tantrums;
- may constantly bump into objects and fall over;
- hands flap when running;
- difficulty with pedalling a tricycle or similar toy;
- lack of any sense of danger (jumping from heights, etc.);
- continued messy eating; may prefer to eat with their fingers, frequently spill drinks;
- avoidance of constructional toys, such as jigsaws or building blocks;
- poor fine motor skills; difficulty in holding a pencil or using scissors; drawings may appear immature;
- lack of imaginative play; may show little interest in dressing up or in playing appropriately in a home corner or Wendy house;
- limited creative play;
- isolation within the peer group; rejected by peers, children may prefer adult company;
- laterality (left- or right-handedness) still not established;
- persistent language difficulties;
- sensitive to sensory stimulation, including high levels of noise, tactile defensiveness, wearing new clothes;
- limited response to verbal instruction; may be slow to respond and have problems with comprehension;
- limited concentration; tasks are often left unfinished.

By 7 years old

Problems may include:

- difficulties in adapting to a structured school routine;
- difficulties in physical education lessons;

- slow at dressing; unable to tie shoe laces;
- barely legible handwriting;
- immature drawing and copying skills;
- limited concentration and poor listening skills;
- literal use of language;
- inability to remember more than two or three instructions at once;
- slow completion of class work;
- continued high levels of motor activity;
- hand flapping or clapping when excited;
- tendency to become easily distressed and emotional;
- problems with coordinating a knife and fork;
- inability to form relationships with other children;
- sleeping difficulties, including wakefulness at night and nightmares;
- reporting of physical symptoms, such as migraine, headaches, feeling sick.

By 8 to 9 years old

- Children with dyspraxia may have become disaffected with the education system. Handwriting is often a particular difficulty. By the time they reach secondary education their attendance record is often poor.

Reflecting on practice

Natasha, aged 11, arrives at the sports hall to carry out her first PE session at the new secondary school she attends. Natasha is unaware of the routine and children seem to be all over the place in the changing rooms, leaving no place for Natasha to go. Natasha is confused about the routine and is afraid to ask the teacher for assistance in case the other children pick on her.

Natasha attempts to change into her sports clothes and a child picks up Natasha's shoe and throws it across the room. Natasha starts to get very anxious and chases the offending child across the room, but due to her problems with gross motor coordination she falls in a heap, crying.

This incident results in Natasha refusing to join in the sporting activity as she is in fear of the other children making fun of her.

This case study highlights the difficulties that may be faced by the child with dyspraxia in what may be considered everyday tasks by other children. It is important to remember here that every child is unique and a child with

→

dyspraxia may need a lot of support in order to function in an educational environment.

Consider the following:

1. How could you have prevented the problems faced by Natasha if you were aware that she had dyspraxia?

2. How could you involve other children and make Natasha feel included?

Identifying dyspraxia in the classroom

It is predominantly parents who tend to notice that a child has difficulties and actively seek a label for these. However, some parents may find this label very detrimental to their child. Ripley et al. (1997, p13) identify the following advantages and disadvantages to being labelled dyspraxic.

Advantages	Disadvantages
1. Parents may contact support agencies to find out more about their child's difficulties and how to help at home	1. The child may be seen as dyspraxic rather than as a unique individual with their own pattern of strengths and weaknesses
2. Information about the condition can be shared with family, friends and teachers	2. A label such as dyspraxia may restrict the expectations that adults have for the child's development
3. The problem may be taken more seriously by professions	3. A label may affect the child's self-perception and self-expectations. Being a special person can be a refuge but it can also be a prison
4. It will help the child's self-esteem to know that he/she is not stupid but does have a recognised problem with which others will help	

Under the *SEN Code* as previously reviewed in Chapter 2, if the teacher has concerns about the child, they will share these with the parent and implement an action plan, adapting the teaching methods in order to assist the child with his/her educational development.

Top tips for identifying dyspraxia in the classroom

- disorganised and very messy books;
- may have a tendency to lose equipment;
- may be unable to find his/her place in a book when reading;

- handwriting is illegible;
- falls over when walking around the classroom;
- often wears shoes on the wrong feet and clothes inside out/back to front;
- when working on practical tasks a very messy approach is adopted; e.g. when painting there is more paint on the table than on the paper;
- easily distracted and draws attention by acting inappropriately;
- finds it very difficult to concentrate;
- makes a mess when eating;
- unable to do more than one task at a time.

The American Psychiatric Association (1994, cited in Macintyre, 2001) sets out five criteria for dyspraxia, the condition they call developmental coordination disorder, as follows:

1. There is a marked impairment in the development of motor coordination.
2. The impairment significantly interferes with academic achievement or activities of daily living.
3. The coordination difficulties are not due to a general medical condition, e.g. cerebral palsy or muscular dystrophy.
4. It is not a pervasive developmental disorder.
5. If a developmental delay is evident, the motor difficulties are in excess of those usually associated with it.

These five criteria may also be used to guide diagnosis of dyspraxia.

Following concerns raised by the teacher, outside professionals including a physiotherapist, an occupational therapist and an educational psychologist will be contacted with a view to conducting an assessment for dyspraxia. As referred to in Chapter 2, in my experience, once a diagnosis has been made, it is essential that the SENCO liaises with all staff concerned and offers guidance and support in order to meet the individual needs of a child with dyspraxia.

Why not try this?

Consider how dyspraxia is identified and assessed in your school and whether training is offered for staff regarding dyspraxia.

How can you ensure that the classroom environment is suitable for a child with dyspraxia?

In order to meet the individual needs of a child who displays characteristics of dyspraxia it is important to consider strategies that may be used in the educational environment. The following list of hints and tips are aimed at teachers/ practitioners working with children who have dyspraxia:

Top tips for teachers/practitioners

In the classroom

- Address the specific needs of the child on a daily basis.
- Ensure that the focus is on the individual child, offering positive reinforcement for small steps (e.g. in PE concentrate on development of skills rather than competitiveness).
- Give consideration to seating in the classroom in order to reduce distractions.
- Avoid asking the child to complete activities that will not meet the child's own interests.
- Avoid distracting displays in the classroom.
- Provide timetables and sequenced instructions to help the learner with organisational skills.
- Offer instructions using language the child can understand and reinforce the instructions with visual prompts such as pictures.

UsefulWebsite

http://www.dyspraxiafoundation.org.uk/services/ed_classroom_guide-lines.php

This website is excellent as it provides classroom guidelines for teaching children with dyspraxia. On the website you can search for examples of potential dyspraxia difficulties that you may come across when working with these children.

Taking part in physical activity

Encourage physical activity taking into account:

- activities that may not require as much hand-eye coordination, including swimming and aerobics;
- the fun element rather than achievement;

● activities that may be broken down into sizeable chunks in order to minimise the pressure placed on the individual to complete a series of tasks.

Writing strategies

● positive reinforcement in order to encourage improvement and participation;
● provide pencil grips, writing lines and stencils to assist with writing tasks.

When working with children displaying characteristics of dyspraxia, I noticed that each child responded to lots and lots of positive reinforcement and a warm, welcoming atmosphere. The importance of listening to the child cannot be underestimated even if it takes a little longer for the child to explain what they are trying to say. We need to be mindful that although dyspraxia is considered a special educational need these children are as able as any other child but have difficulties in areas such as movement, coordination, planning and organising. Thus, it is very important that educators take into account the individual needs of the child and have regular communication with parents in order to ensure a consistent approach to managing the difficulties faced by the child.

The learning environment

When in the learning environment simple adaptations are needed. Specialist equipment such as writing frames, whereby the child is able to follow a structured framework to write about a specific subject, will make a huge difference to the learning experience of the child. And by ensuring that distractions are reduced wherever possible the child is more likely to have an uninterrupted lesson and find it much easier to concentrate on the task at hand.

It is important to provide a visual timetable for the child so that he/she is aware of the routine for the day, which may consist of pictures to assist the child in understanding everyday routines. An alarm clock is also a useful tool to demonstrate how much time the child has left on a specific test.

Teaching strategies

When preparing to teach it is vital that the preferred learning style of the child is taken into consideration; and when planning activities try to offer these in the child's preferred learning style. Break down the tasks into sizeable chunks to prevent overloading the child with information which will only confuse and irritate him/her due to possible problems with short-term memory. It may be necessary to repeat tasks on several occasions before the child is able to learn the information.

Many activities in the classroom will be difficult and frustrating for the child with dyspraxia. Planning a task will be a huge stepping stone. Consider how you would organise a task for a child who has dyspraxia.

Conclusion

Many teachers as they understand the complexities of dyspraxia are able to appreciate the behaviour displayed by these children, which is often inappropriate due to their frustrations and everyday difficulties experienced in the learning environment. By enabling these children using the practical strategies demonstrated in this chapter, their lives may be transformed both in school and in the wider community.

Key ideas summary

- Think about what you have learnt about dyspraxia.
- What are the key characteristics of dyspraxia?
- What symptoms may be present that will make identification possible?
- How do teachers determine if a child in your class has dyspraxia?
- Does the teacher use a checklist to record any difficulties that may be apparent in relation to gross/fine motor skills, coordination and organisational skills?
- What strategies are put in place to enable the child with dyspraxia to progress in the learning environment?
- What are the most important things to consider when in the classroom with a pupil who has dyspraxia?

Going further

References and further reading

Dyspraxic Foundation (2009) *Supporting Children, Families and Adults with Dyspraxia*, http://www.dyspraxiafoundation.org.uk/, accessed June 2009.

Macintyre, C. (2001) *Dyspraxia 5–11*, London: David Fulton.

Pollock, J., Waller, E. and Politt, R. (2004) *Day-to-day Dyslexia in the Classroom*, London: Routledge Falmer.

Ripley, K., Daines, B. and Barrett, J. (1997) *Dyspraxia: A Guide for Teachers and Parents*, London: David Fulton

Thomson, M. (2003) *Dyslexia Included: A Whole School Approach*, London: David Fulton.

Autistic spectrum disorder (ASD)

What this chapter will explore:

- Theories and key characteristics of autism
- Identifying autism in the classroom
- The TEACCH approach
- Hints and tips for teachers

This chapter will provide an insight into the theories of autism and the key characteristics of this special educational need. The aim of the chapter is to ensure that teachers gain an understanding of the complex nature of autistic spectrum disorder (ASD) and are aware of strategies that may be used to assist them in ensuring an inclusive approach to teaching children who are on the autistic spectrum.

Theories and key characteristics of autism

Although autism has existed throughout history Leo Kanner, a child psychiatrist, was the first person to formally identify autism as a set of characteristics in 1943 in his paper 'Autistic disturbance of affective contact'. Kanner defined the features of autism as follows:

- a profound autistic withdrawal
- an obsessive desire for the preservation of sameness
- a good rote memory
- an intelligent and pensive expression
- mutism, or language without real communicative intent
- over-sensitivity to stimuli
- a skilful relationship to objects.

(Cumine et al., 2000, p1)

This breakthrough in understanding children who had previously received no help was considered very important in meeting the needs of any child who displayed characteristics of autism (Cumine et al., 2000, p1).

Following this, Wing (1996, cited in Plimley and Bowen, 2006) defined autism as a development difficulty that combines:

- impairment with social communication
- impairment with social interaction
- impairment with social imagination.

Without this triad of impairments the individual would not be diagnosed as autistic. These difficulties tend to be severe and learning difficulties are also often present.

Social interaction

For the majority of people, social interaction is an everyday part of life and most people are able to interact with others without any problems, reading body language and making eye contact in order to add meaning to communication. Body language, facial signals and eye contact tend to offer meaningful information and we are able to read facial signs very easily.

In contrast a person who is on the autism spectrum may be unable to read body language, facial signs and eye contact and as a result may become very confused with what may seem simple to the majority of people. It is important to remember that each individual on the autism spectrum may use eye contact very differently. It may be that some individuals gaze into space, and others are unable to follow subtle signals with regard to how a person is feeling emotionally.

Imitation skills

While children who do not have autism may imitate others when they are in an unfamiliar situation, the majority of children with autism will be unaware of what others are doing around them. They may imitate other children without realising why they are doing this, and may imitate children who quite clearly are not good role models as they are unable to understand what social expectations are in different environmental contexts.

Social imagination

As a child on the autism spectrum has difficulties with social imagination they find it very difficult to understand and accept changes to routines. Their inflexibility of thought causes them great distress when changes are made and thus the school environment is a very difficult place due to:

● regular changes in classroom routines

● changes in the classroom environment

● changing schools

● changes in lessons.

A child with autism also finds it very difficult to play in the way that other children play as he/she would not be able to use their imagination in the same way. In my experience of working with children with autism, each and every one plays with toys in a very repetitive way, using little imagination. A child may become obsessed with certain toys and find it hard to make the transition from playing with a toy to working on a literacy task. This is because the child who has autism is unable to understand the structure of the transition period and predict what may come next. Bearing this in mind the transition from lesson to lesson may cause great distress for a child with autism.

Language and communication

A child who has autism differs very much from other children in relation to language and communication as they may have language processing difficulties and find comprehension hard. These children may be able to process language and understand what it means, but they interpret language in literal terms. For example, when teaching a child with autism in a cookery lesson a few years ago

I asked him to pour boiling water onto gravy granules and he poured the water straight into the packet of gravy granules and on to the floor. Another example is that when saying to a child, 'It's raining cats and dogs' we need to be mindful that as a child with autism only understands language in the literal sense, this expression will confuse them as they are unable to interpret it and will often see the visual representation, which quite clearly does not make sense!

The issues of autism are very complex and some individuals on the autistic spectrum will display **echolalia**, which means they repeat what they have heard even though they do not understand the content. It is therefore very important as a teacher to consider instructions and ensure that they are clear and meaningful. As some children who have severe autism may have very little verbal communication they may use echolalia in order to communicate how they are feeling or to gain a rapport with a member of staff. An example of this from my own experience was when working with a pupil in a secondary school recently, who when asked if he would like to do some gardening would respond 'Stuart likes gardening' even though he did not know what gardening was and had never experienced it. If I suggested doing something new, this pupil would respond to what I asked him to do by saying 'Stuart likes ...' over and over again.

Plimley and Bowen (2006, p4–5) offer the following common characteristics of autistic spectrum disorder as a guideline for teachers/practitioners in the classroom.

Communication

- lack of speech
- limited conversation
- speech likely to develop more slowly than is the norm for children of the same age
- unable to respond spontaneously
- unable to share social situations
- lack of desire to communicate.

Social interaction

- unable to form social bonds
- avoids eye contact
- limited play skills
- inability to understand others' thinking
- inability to understand others' feelings
- difficulty with tolerating peers.

Social imagination

- unable to use own imagination to create pictures
- unable to understand jokes
- has difficulty in initiating play with other children
- may prefer to be left alone
- lack of imitation of other individuals' actions.

UsefulWebsite

http://www.nas.org.uk/nas/jsp/polopoly.jsp?d=211&a=13432

This is an excellent website for finding out more about autistic spectrum disorder. There are useful links to research articles.

The cause of autism still remains unknown. However, it appears that there is no single cause, but there may be triggers which occur and cause autism. What is known is that autism is a physical disorder of the brain, that causes a lifelong developmental disability, and boys are more likely to be affected than girls. Approximately 1 in 100 people are believed to have ASD (Baird et al., 2006, cited in Bowen and Plimley, 2008), although it is very difficult to gauge how many people have ASD as it is not always easy to identify. Some people may go through life and cope without any additional support and help, whereas others may receive a diagnosis in adulthood and gain support from this time onwards. Each individual with ASD is unique and may present the disability in very different ways and with different degrees of severity. Quite often ASD may be associated with other difficulties, including dyspraxia, dyslexia, attention deficit hyperactivity disorder, obsessive compulsive disorder and epilepsy. What is clear is that all individuals with ASD demonstrate the triad of impairments proposed by Wing.

Individuals within the spectrum may also be described as having:

- Asperger syndrome
- high-functioning autism
- classical autism
- Kanner's autism.

It is clear that people with autism perceive the world in a very different way; for example, an autistic child may walk into a room full of people and not appear to notice them. Behaviours including 'twiddling' may be demonstrated by the child and some children with ASD develop obsessive interests in certain toys or objects. One example of this was a child who had ASD with whom I worked at a local special school who was obsessed with 'Thomas the Tank Engine'. In order to motivate this child, lots of resources were developed around this theme, although at times this presented problems as the child found it very hard to engage in anything other than Thomas the Tank Engine.

Identifying autism in the classroom

When identifying autism the following check list may be useful:

- difficulties in communication, resulting in poor use of language, both receptive and expressive;
- child may refuse to show interest in any individual;
- child does not develop speech even at the age of three;
- child appears to be unaware of other people in the room and does not interact with anyone;
- child fails to make eye contact;
- child rocks and twiddles hands;
- child may be highly sensitive to smells, food, noises;
- child may echo conversations rather than respond correctly and may interpret a conversation literally.

It is clear that even if a formal diagnosis of autism has not been made, any child who displays the characteristics of the triad of impairments will need an individualised and specialised programme of education, tailored to meet the child's specific needs.

Reflecting on practice

Adam is a four-year-old boy who has severe ASD and severe learning difficulties. He has just started school and is unfamiliar with his new surroundings, which is causing him a great deal of distress. Adam is unable to communicate verbally and uses picture symbols to aid him. When he becomes agitated he throws his symbols across the room and has an outburst of very aggressive behaviour towards staff. Adam's behaviour is very inconsistent. One minute he can be happy and the next, for no apparent reason, he becomes distressed and agitated, throwing any object within his reach across the room and hitting anyone who approaches him. Adam's lack of understanding of the routines of the day is causing him to have outbursts of screaming and yelling and he has resorted to kicking chairs.

→

This case study highlights the issues that a child on the autism spectrum may face when starting a new school. It is clear from Adam's story that communication can be very difficult for an individual with autism and the outbursts of behaviour demonstrated are his way of communicating his unhappiness with his new situation. Adam is clearly excluded from the educational environment due to his autistic traits, and he is finding it very difficult to cope with the transition into school.

Consider the following:

1. Is there a child in your class who demonstrates characteristics like Adam's?
2. What does the child find calming to do?
3. If there is a change in routine, does the child become distressed?
4. What strategies are put in place to assist the child in remaining calm?

We need to remember that children who are autistic find it very difficult to adapt to any change in their routines, and this makes the educational environment very challenging. Children with autism are often unable to make sense of what many activities they take part in mean, and they are unable to generalise to the situation appropriately. For example, they don't realise that it is not appropriate to take your clothes off in a shop and yet it is fine to do this in the bedroom. This obviously causes many problems in the school environment, as there are many changes in routine on a daily basis including changes of staff and changes in times lessons finish. For Adam these minute changes cause heightened anxiety as he is unable to cope with the concept of change, hence his outbursts of aggressive behaviour.

People with autism generally have problems with over-stimulation and this may lead to erratic behaviour in the classroom, as the child with autism may also be very sensitive to noise, touch, smell, movement, lights, food and sunlight. Classrooms are often too noisy, very active and full of clutter. If a person who has autism is touched unexpectedly it may feel as if they were receiving an electric shock. It is useful to bear all these problems in mind when considering how to best work with a child with autism.

It is useful at this point to draw on an analogy presented by Tony Attwood (Attwood, 1998, cited in Hesmondalgh and Breakey, 2001, p17). Attwood uses the analogy of a brick wall to stress that every single part of life for the individual with autism has to be in place in order for progression to occur. If one brick is missing, this impacts on the whole structure of the wall. It is the same for a child with autism, and if one part of the structure of the child's life is missing, the impact is tremendous.

It is imperative that there is effective teamwork between teachers, teaching assistants (TAs), SENCOs and parents in order to contribute to the effective teaching of a child with autism. With this in mind, we will now consider the importance of structuring the classroom environment in order to meet the needs of a child on the autism spectrum.

Research evidence

Eric Schopler, an American psychologist, conducted research into autism and as a result founded the Treatment and Education of Autistic and Communication-handicapped Children (TEACCH) programme in the early 1970s. This programme is widely used and focuses on developing highly structured settings for learning, specifically drawing on an individual's skills, interests and needs. The structured TEACCH approach includes physical organisation, daily schedules and work systems.

The TEACCH approach

The TEACCH programme is international in its scope and has been very successful in providing a structured approach for a child with autism in order that they are able to cope with the changing environment of the school (Mesibov et al., 2006).

Physical organisation

The majority of children with autism will find it very distracting and disturbing if the classroom is not structured, as physical organisation offers boundaries for a child with autism and also minimises distractions and other stimulants that will take him/her away from their focus of work. Physical structure also offers contextual cues in order that the child can make sense of their world, for example; consistently placing specific items in the same place. Failure to provide these clues causes further anxiety for the child.

Daily schedules

Some of the ways we can manage challenging behaviours to try and help a child with autism are by providing a clear structure to each day, offering clear beginnings and endings for each given session or task. These may be provided by way of pictures and/or words depending on the individual needs of the child. Some children may even require a system whereby, when a task is complete, they remove the word or picture from the schedule in order to understand that they have finished the task. Daily schedules are also useful as a vehicle to provide a link to concrete experience, for example a picture of a knife, fork and plate may indicate that it is time to eat. This is very important as the individual with autism often relies on visual stimuli in order to associate actions with images.

Work systems

Work systems enable a child with autism to have a systematic way of working. These may include written work systems, which offer written instructions to reinforce what needs to be done, and matching systems, where the pupil is expected to match a number to a task to show that this work is complete. It is important to use whatever method is preferred, as a child with autism will only engage with material that motivates them.

UsefulWebsite

http://www.nas.org.uk/nas/jsp/polopoly.jsp?d=297&a=3630

This website provides an overview of the TEACCH programme and gives useful contacts and publications in relation to the TEACCH approach.

Why not try this?

Answer the following questions to reinforce your learning about the TEACCH programme:

- What are the three main focuses of the TEACCH programme?
- Think about how you could create physical conditions in your classroom that will help a child with autism understand the context more clearly.

Mary Pittman (2007, p75) offers the following audit of the school/classroom environment to assist you with planning for a child with autism.

Audit of the school/classroom environment

Feature	Level of current or potential intervention
Seating arrangements	• Pupil is flexible in where he/she sits for each lesson of activity and displays no behaviours or anxieties related to his/her seating place but requires verbal direction where to sit • Pupil could/does benefit from a designated place to sit for each lesson or activity • Pupil could/does benefit from a level of seating boundary to minimise distractions • Pupil could/does benefit from seating areas to move to in the classroom which demonstrate that working arrangements are used only for a set purpose e.g. independent workstation • Pupil could/does benefit from moving his/her own chair to and from different areas as a means of individually structuring classroom movement to areas • Pupil could/does benefit from an independent working base as a main seating place with movement to and from that base for specific lesson activity only.
Calm areas	• Pupil could/does benefit from time using a specific calm area of the classroom or school and can take himself/herself there as needed • Pupil could/does benefit from regular direction from staff to move to a specified calm area of the classroom • Pupil could/does benefit from regular timetabled use of a specified calm area for short periods • Pupil could/does benefit from spending more extensive time in a specified calm area for parts of the day or week known to be problematic.
Areas to use in break or lunchtime	• Pupil could/does benefit from being directed to specific areas of the playground • Pupil could/does benefit from using a special interest activity during break time • Pupil could/does benefit from using a break-time quiet area, or a special break-time club.
Sensory considerations	• Consider any features of the learning environment that cause the pupil difficulties with sensory overload, e.g.: strip lights, windows, computer screens, noisy equipment, noisy peers, next to a radiator.

Hints and tips for teachers

In order to support a child on the autistic spectrum we need to recognise the individual needs of the child. There have been many changes over recent years, and following the introduction of the *SEN Code*, many individuals with special educational needs are included in mainstream schools wherever possible. Prior to this legislation being introduced, the principle was quite the opposite: the child with a Statement of Special Education would in most cases be placed in a special school. As a result of the *SEN Code* a child with SEN must now have a clear case that his or her needs may not be met in a mainstream school in order to be educated in a special school. This clearly has implications for the staff teaching a child with autism in relation to meeting their individual needs effectively, as predominantly the mainstream teacher will not have received any training in order to develop knowledge of autism. Pittman (2007, p26) offers the following suggestions for helping children with autism to learn:

- Develop a broad knowledge of autism.
- Develop an understanding of each individual's unique autism profile.
- Recognise the range of features and the presentation of features within each area of the triad of impairment.
- Focus on the learning strengths of a child with autism.
- Use difficulties as opportunities for understanding autism and for supporting adults in modifying interactions and communication in order to be effective.
- Recognise and prepare for our role as 'cross-cultural interpreter'.

In addition to the suggestions made by Pittman the following hints and tips are offered as a support mechanism for teachers or practitioners working with a child with autism.

Consistency

It is essential that all individuals in a supporting role, including teachers, TAs and SENCOs, offer a consistent approach by communicating clearly the expectations for the day using language that can be understood by the child.

Understanding

When working with children who are on the autistic spectrum it is crucial that you understand behaviours which may be related to attempts to communicate, including aggressive behaviour. A child with autism often displays this aggressive behaviour in front of those who have the closest relationship with him/her.

It is important not to take any comments made by the child personally as they will tell you what they see, for example if they think you have a big nose they will say so! The child will need extensive support to assist them in understanding why these comments are not appropriate. A simple way of doing this is by having a happy face and a sad face symbol card and showing this at the appropriate times.

Reducing anxiety

As teachers and educators we need to be mindful that even the slightest change in routine causes major anxiety for a child with autism. We need to put strategies in place to minimise disruption in the routine of the child, but where it is not possible to stop the changes taking place the use of symbols or clear instructions will enable the child to deal with the changes more appropriately. You also need to be aware of signs and triggers of anxiety and provide a way of taking the child away from the situation (for example a favourite toy to use as a distraction).

Behaviour

When a child who has autism displays inappropriate behaviour it is often because he/she is having difficulty communicating and thus it is important to assess the behaviours as and when they occur in the following way:

● What occurs prior to the behaviour to trigger the actions the child takes?
● What behaviour is the child displaying?
● When and where does it occur and how often?
● How do staff intervene?
● What is the consequence of the behaviour for the child?

In order to minimise inappropriate behaviour it is important to ensure that distractions in the classroom are reduced to a minimum. It may be useful to provide the child with his/her workstation and ensure that short breaks are timetabled into the daily routine too.

UsefulWebsite

http://www.speechlanguagepractice.org/?q=node/108

This is an excellent website for more information focusing on the use of video to teach emotions to autistic children.

Social skills

As children with autism find social interaction very difficult it is the responsibility of the teacher or educator to ensure that the classroom environment has clear areas defined where social interaction may take place, and also a quiet area for individual work.

The children may find it very difficult to articulate their emotions, and the use of media including videos of themselves may assist with developing their understanding of emotions.

Raising awareness

It is essential that all staff working with a child on the autistic spectrum have a broad understanding of the child's needs in order to ensure that a consistent approach is offered throughout the day.

Why not try this?

Think about your own learning environment and any child who displays the characteristics of autism. Use the following checklist provided by Seach et al. (2002, p24) to assess how you meet the individual needs of this child.

Personal factors	
The ability of the child – their strengths and weaknesses	
The developmental level of the child and any emerging skills	
Communication skills, e.g. receptive and expressive language use	
Independence skills	
Personality	
Interests	
Social factors	
How does the child relate to adults and peers?	
Do they prefer to be alone?	
How do they behave in a group?	
How do they respond to the learning environment?	
Are they easily distracted?	
Behaviour	
What types of behaviours are displayed?	
Are there any aggressive or self-injurious behaviours?	
When and where do the behaviours occur?	
What is the nature of obsessional interests?	
What is their reaction to intervention?	

A structured approach

The use of embedded structures wherever possible is vital in order to provide an effective learning experience for a child with autism. By making the environment as predictable as possible the child may be able to cope more easily and telling the child what is going to happen, and when, may reduce his/her anxiety levels. It is important to recognise any trigger behaviours and introduce strategies to minimise them.

Language

When working with a child who has autism provide simple, clear instructions and ensure you communicate at a level the child is able to understand. You may need to use symbols or pictures to help the child understand what is required of him/her. It is also important to offer opportunities throughout the day whereby language can be developed (for example through play).

Conclusion

When looking at managing the learning of a child who is on the autistic spectrum it is clear that a structured routine is of paramount importance to the individual. Identification and assessment at an early stage of education are also essential in order that suitable strategies may be put in place to support the child in achieving his/her educational goals and preparing him/her for life in the wider community.

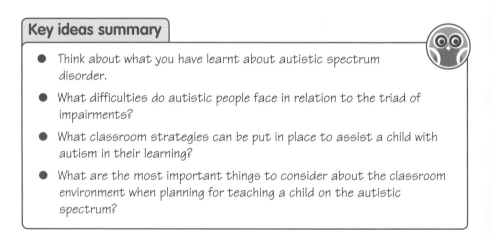

Key ideas summary

- Think about what you have learnt about autistic spectrum disorder.
- What difficulties do autistic people face in relation to the triad of impairments?
- What classroom strategies can be put in place to assist a child with autism in their learning?
- What are the most important things to consider about the classroom environment when planning for teaching a child on the autistic spectrum?

Going further

References and further reading

Baird, G., Simonoff, E., Pickles, A. et al. (2006) 'Prevalence of Disorders or the Autism Spectrum in a Population Cohort of Children in South Thames: The Special Needs and Autism Project (SNAP)', *Lancet*, 368: 210–5.

Bowen, M. and Plimley, L. (2008) *The Autism Inclusion Toolkit*, London: Sage.

Cumine, V., Leach, J. and Stevenson, G. (2000) *Autism in the Early Years: A Practical Guide*, London: David Fulton.

Hesmondalgh, M. and Breakey, C. (2001) *Access and Inclusion for Children with Autistic Spectrum Disorders: 'Let Me In'*, London: Jessica Kingsley.

Kanner, L. (1943) 'Autistic Disturbances of Affective Contact in Nervous Child', 2: 217–50.

Mesibov, G.B., Shea, V. and Schopler, E. (2006) *The TEACCH Approach to Autism Spectrum Disorders*, New York: Springer.

Pittman, M. (2007) *Helping Pupils with Autistic Spectrum Disorders to Learn*, London: Sage.

Plimley, L. and Bowen, M. (2006) *Supporting Pupils with Autistic Spectrum Disorders*, London: Sage.

Seach, D., Lloyd, M. and Preston, M. (2002) *Supporting Children with Autism in Mainstream Schools*, Birmingham: Questions Publishing.

Hearing impairment

What this chapter will explore:

- Hearing impairment
- Identifying hearing impairments
- The learning environment
- Hints and tips for teachers

This chapter concentrates on children who have hearing impairments. It considers different types of hearing loss and the consequences of this for the child when in the educational environment. The aim of this chapter is to equip teachers and practitioners to identify any possible difficulties a child may have with hearing and to suggest different strategies for ensuring the successful integration of such a child.

Hearing impairment

Children who have hearing difficulties represent the second largest group of children with special educational needs in the UK (Stakes and Hornby, 2000). Hearing impairment or deafness occurs as a result of a disease, disorder or injury (National Health Service, 2009).

The ear consists of three parts: the outer ear, the middle ear and the inner ear. The outer ear is the part of the ear visible on the side of your head. The eardrum is the start of the middle ear, which vibrates when sound hits it. These vibrations travel from the eardrum on to three small bones called the ossicles that amplify the sounds and pass them through to the inner ear. The inner ear contains the cochlea, which transfers the vibrations along the auditory nerve whence they are perceived by the brain (see Figure 8.1).

These vibrations are passed to the cochlea where they are transmitted as electrical signals that the brain then decodes.

There are two types of hearing impairment:

1. Conductive hearing loss – caused when something such as wax or 'glue ear' blocks the ear which results in a collection of fluid in the ear when a child has a heavy cold. This is often treated and hearing is restored to normal limits.

2. Sensorineural hearing loss – caused when there is a problem with the inner ear, or the pathway from the inner ear to the brain. This is more serious and

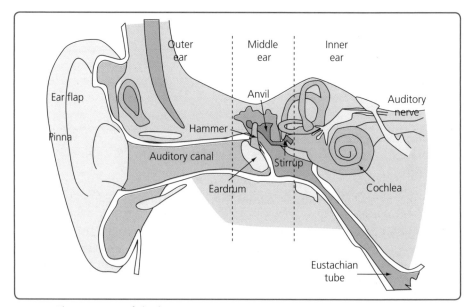

Fig 8.1: The structure of the human ear

hearing is not usually restored to normal limits. This necessitates wearing a hearing aid to produce amplification of sound; however, sound is somewhat distorted as a result.

RNID (2009a) definitions of deafness

- **Mild deafness** – Mild deafness can cause some difficulty following speech, mainly in noisy situations. The quietest sounds that can be heard are 25–39 decibels.

- **Moderate deafness** – People with moderate deafness may have difficulty following speech without a hearing aid, and find the quietest sounds they can hear are 40–69 decibels.

- **Severe deafness** – People with severe deafness rely a lot on lip reading, even with a hearing aid, as the quietest sounds they can hear are 70–94 decibels. British Sign Language (BSL) may be their first or preferred language.

- **Profound deafness** – The quietest sounds that profoundly deaf people can hear average 95 decibels or more. BSL may be their first or preferred language but some prefer to lip read.

UsefulWebsite

http://www.rnid.org.uk/information_resources/aboutdeafness/ meaning_of_deafness/

This website is operated by the leading charity for deaf and hearing-impaired people. It is a useful site from which to obtain information about the different types of deafness. There are useful links to theory and research surrounding this impairment.

Research evidence

RNID estimates that there are almost 9 million deaf and hearing-impaired people in the UK (RNIDa, 2009). Statistics from RNID suggest that approximately 840 babies are born each year in the UK with significant deafness and one in 1,000 children is deaf at 3 years old. There are approximately 20,000 children aged 0–15 who are moderately to profoundly deaf, and there are approximately 12,000 children aged 0–15 who were born deaf (RNIDb, 2009).

Identifying hearing impairments

Depending on the severity of hearing impairment the child may be educated in a mainstream environment with the offer of additional support. However, a very small number of children who are severely or profoundly deaf may be educated in a special school for deaf children as they need specialised support in the form of British Sign Language to enable them to communicate effectively.

From my experience of working with children who have hearing problems, the following behaviours may be indicators that a child is having difficulty with his/her hearing:

- asking for information to be repeated on a regular basis and finding listening very difficult
- finding it hard to hear clearly in noisy classroom situations
- talking in a loud voice
- not responding when spoken to
- developing speech very slowly
- being unable to speak clearly
- pressing on ear frequently.

Why not try this?

If you suspect a child may have hearing problems use the following questions to decide whether or not to refer the child for an evaluation of their hearing:

- Is the child progressing at a similar rate to his/her hearing peers?
- Is the child displaying any characteristics that are not usually seen with a mainstream child, such as inability to learn vocabulary, memory problems, distractive behaviours?

Reflecting on practice

Katie is seven years old and attends her local primary school. She has suffered with ear infection after ear infection from the age of two. She has difficulty reading and writing, and when Katie's parents approached the teacher about these problems the teacher compared Katie with her older brother who was a very able child. Katie finds it very difficult to listen in class and is easily distracted by visual or auditory stimuli. She tends to withdraw from any classroom activities that involve listening. Katie is always in trouble

→

for ignoring the teacher when asked a question and she always asks for information to be repeated.

Consider the following:

1. Is there a child in your class who demonstrates characteristics like Katie's?

2. How do you monitor these difficulties and what action have you taken to ascertain if the child has hearing problems?

3. What strategies have you put in place to assist the child with his/her hearing problems?

Children with hearing impairment may present a challenge to teachers and practitioners in the mainstream environment. These children will all have varying degrees of deafness and as such their support needs will vary tremendously.

Why not try this?

Consider the difference in the educational needs of a child with mild hearing loss to those of a child with severe hearing loss. How would you cater for each child in the learning environment?

The learning environment

It is important to ensure the appropriate learning environment is available for every child, including those with a hearing impairment. From my own practice I draw on the following key points to assist me when planning the environment.

Physical environment

● Ensure that the child is seated in the best possible place to facilitate his/her learning.

● Ensure that the child has sight of the teacher in order that he/she can lip read.

● Ensure that the teacher is positioned in order to face the child when communicating.

● If an interpreter is to be used make sure that the child is seated so that they can see the interpreter.

It is also important to provide an appropriate acoustic environment. This may be gained by using the following modifications.

Acoustic environment

- fitted carpets
- thick curtains/blinds
- covers on chair and table legs in order to reduce the amount of excessive noise in the room.

Hints and tips for teachers

The following hints and tips are useful when teaching children with hearing impairments:

- Plan lessons with pupils' aural needs in mind.
- Always ensure that pupils can see your face when you are talking in the classroom.
- Speak clearly and slowly.
- Rephrase explanations and instructions wherever necessary, providing key words on the whiteboard.
- Use sign language communication aids including British Sign Language and electronic aids wherever necessary.
- Use visual cues to assist with presentations.
- Write information on the whiteboard.
- Use facial expressions and gestures when talking.
- Always check that students understand what has been communicated by asking questions.
- Use visual aids to explain tasks.
- Allow students to use computers for word processing their work.

Why not try this?

Identify a lesson that you have already planned and consider how you need to adapt the resources for this lesson in order to cater for a pupil with a hearing impairment.

Prior to planning the lesson think about the following:

- The child's interests.
- Which teaching methods work best with the child?
- How can you facilitate opportunities for developing the child's independence?
- How can you best facilitate the learning of the child?

There are also various materials that may be used to assist hearing-impaired pupils:

- assistive listening devices (hearing aids)
- computer-assisted note taking
- induction loops
- cochlear implants.

Conclusion

Recognising that hearing-impaired pupils will find it very difficult to associate with the 'hearing' culture is the first step to ensuring an inclusive educational environment. It is essential that these pupils have equal opportunities and become an integral part of the inclusive school community, as failure to do this may result in them becoming very withdrawn and isolated. The aim of teachers, practitioners and parents is to provide an inclusive environment for all pupils, and with this in mind it is important to recognise the importance of putting strategies in place to ensure each and every pupil is accepted regardless of any special educational need that may be apparent.

Key ideas summary

- Think about what you have learnt about hearing impairment.
- How might you recognise that a pupil has a hearing impairment?
- What strategies can you put into place in the classroom to ensure that the learner who is deaf reaches his/her maximum learning potential?
- What are the most important things to consider about the classroom environment when planning for teaching a child with a hearing impairment?

Going further

References and further reading

National Health Service (2009) *Hearing Impairment*, http://www.nhs.uk/
Conditions/Hearing-impairment/Pages/Introduction.aspx accessed
July 2009.

Peer, L. (2005) *Glue Ear: An Essential Guide for Teachers, Parents and
Health Professionals*, London: David Fulton.

RNIDa (2009) *Information and Resources*, http://www.rnid.org.uk/
information_resources/, accessed July 2009.

RNIDb (2009) *Statistics*, http://www.rnid.org.uk/information_resources/
aboutdeafness/statistics/statistics.htm#deaf, accessed July 2009.

Stakes, R. and Hornby, G. (2000) (2nd edn) *Meeting Special Needs in
Mainstream Schools: A Practical Guide for Teachers*, London: David
Fulton.

Visual impairment

This chapter will offer an overview of the term visual impairment and an understanding of the importance of ensuring that children with visual impairments receive particular attention in relation to their education. The aim of this chapter is to equip teachers with strategies that may be used in the classroom when working with children with visual impairments. It is essential to ensure that the individual child's educational needs are met and an inclusive approach is offered for the child to be successful and reach his/her maximum educational potential.

What is visual impairment?

The term visual impairment is used to describe any individual who may be blind or partially sighted, in contrast to being short-sighted or long-sighted (National Health Service, 2009). There are two conditions referred to if an individual is visually impaired: partial sightedness and blindness.

Partial sightedness – refers to a person who is partially sighted or has very low vision. The World Health Organisation defines a partially sighted person as someone who is unable to see how many fingers are being held up at a distance of 19 feet or less, even if they are wearing glasses or contact lenses.

Blindness – refers to a person who has severe sight loss and will be unable to see how many fingers are being held up at a distance of 9.8 feet or less, even if wearing glasses or lenses. The majority of people who are considered blind do have some sight.

Poor acuity – This term relates to the clarity or sharpness of the overall image. Both distance and near vision may be affected and some individuals may be able to see close work but not be able to see a whiteboard, whereas others may find it hard to see close work yet easy to read from a whiteboard.

Central vision loss – This prevents the individual from seeing fine detail and is likely to affect work such as reading, writing and often close work.

Peripheral vision loss – In contrast to central vision loss, this may result in tunnel-like field vision and individuals may experience difficulty moving around the classroom and finding specific objects.

Adapted from Salisbury, 2008

There are several different eye conditions including the following:

Cataracts – cause temporary blindness; however they can be surgically removed.

Glaucoma – causes temporary blindness, which can be treated with eye drops or surgery.

Injury or trauma to the eyes

Abnormal blood vessel growth following premature birth and diabetes.

Macular degeneration – this is a common cause of reduced vision, which is as a result of wear and tear of the eye. It tends to be more prevalent as a person ages. This condition does not cause total blindness as only the central field of vision is affected.

Genetic conditions

It is important to remember that although the definition of visual impairment may be considered useful in order to claim special entitlements, there are many different eye conditions and as a result sight can be affected in many different ways (Davis, 2003).

One individual who is considered blind may have peripheral vision, whereas another person may also be considered blind and have tunnel vision, and yet another person may only have the ability to see in certain levels of light.

Functional vision is a very important term as it refers to what an individual may see and how a specialist may optimise the sight available to a child by assisting him/her in making the best use of functional vision (Davis, 2003). The specialist will liaise with the classroom teacher and any other staff working with the child to ensure they are able to help in the best possible way.

Mason and McCall (1997, cited in Davis, 2003) advocate using the term 'visual impairment' to describe a continuum of sight loss. They suggest that the term 'blind' should be used to describe an individual who relies heavily on tactile methods in learning, specifically Braille.

Research evidence

The proportion of children with visual impairments in mainstream schools at the time of writing is unknown. However, given the emphasis placed on inclusive education children with visual impairments are increasingly likely to be educated in a mainstream environment (Davis, 2003). A decision with regard to the individual child's education will be made as a result of negotiations between parents and the local authority, as it is important that the child receives the type of provision suitable for his/her needs. The Centre for Studies in Inclusive Education (CSIE) provides a definition of inclusive education in Index for Inclusion (http://www.csie.org.uk/publications/inclusion-index-explained.shtml) (Booth and Ainscow, 2002, cited in Salisbury, 2008) suggesting that inclusive education means children and young people with disabilities and those without learn together in ordinary pre-school provision, schools, colleges and universities, with appropriate networks of support. With this in mind it is the responsibility of the local authority/school to adapt the educational environment to meet the needs of the child with visual impairment.

Identifying visual impairments

Predominantly a child with visual impairment will have been diagnosed prior to starting school during routine visits to the child development clinic, or they may have been identified as visually impaired shortly after birth while still in hospital. It is clear that visual skills are very important to the learning process as without these skills the individual may have difficulties in learning to read. On the whole children with visual difficulties are partially sighted and may be educated in a mainstream school environment. However, a very small proportion are totally blind and tend to be educated in special schools to ensure they receive the appropriate support.

From my experience of working with pupils who have visual impairments, the following characteristics may be demonstrated:

- clumsiness
- poor hand-eye coordination
- holding the head in an unusual way
- frowning, making faces or squinting more often than normal
- complaining of headaches or dizziness
- having poorly formed handwriting
- having difficulty in seeing the whiteboard/flipchart
- becoming tired more quickly than other children.

If a child demonstrates any of these characteristics and you suspect there are difficulties a full medical diagnosis is important to ensure that the educational needs and sight needs of a child are met.

Children are screened for visual problems in the educational environment and if a problem is suspected a further examination will take place. This examination is used to assess visual acuity and field of vision. Visual acuity will be evaluated using a Snellen Chart (see Figure 9.1)

If an individual is identified as having vision problems at this stage they would be referred to opthalmologists, medical doctors and optometrists (who evaluate vision and prescribe glasses).

To ascertain your field of vision an optometrist tests how much you can see around the edge of your vision while looking straight ahead.

UsefulWebsite

http://www.rnib.org.uk/xpedio/groups/public/documents/publicwebsite/public_cert_vi.hcsp

This website is useful if you wish to find out more about the Snellen test and how an eye consultant measures eyes. It also provides links to useful sites for anyone who is concerned about their eyesight.

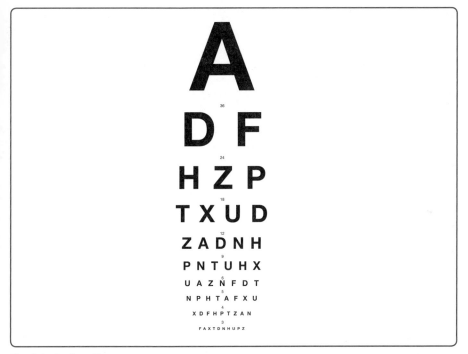

Fig 9.1: Snellen Chart

Why not try this?

If you suspect a child has a visual impairment observe the child and use the following checklist to note your concerns. (The list is adapted from Hallahan and Kauffman (2003, cited in Smith et al., 2008, p323.)

- Has difficulty in reading or in other work that requires close use of the eyes.
- Blinks more often than usual.
- Holds books very close to eyes.
- Is unable to see things at a distance clearly.
- Cannot see well.
- Suffers from headaches or nausea following close eye work.
- Blurred or double vision.

Reflecting on practice

Rizwan is six years old and has just started to attend his local primary school. He is very popular with his classmates but unlike the rest of his class Rizwan is very clumsy and appears to trip over everything when moving around the classroom. When working on writing tasks, Rizwan is unable to form any letters and always complains about the writing on the whiteboard being unclear. As a result he seems easily distracted and lacks concentration. Rizwan tends to tilt his head to one side when he moves around the classroom.

Consider the following:

1. How could you adapt the environment to suit Rizwan's needs?
2. How can you help other children to understand the importance of keeping the classroom free from obstructions?
3. How will you adapt resources to assist Rizwan with his learning?

It is important to recognise that visually impaired children who attend a mainstream school may require a wide range of support. Recently I worked with a young woman at a special school who was visually impaired and she needed one-to-one support throughout her day at school. She used Braille to communicate and thus it was important that staff members were trained to read Braille. Specialist resources were supplied including educational resources and games in order that the pupil was included. The food technology room was adapted and Braille stickers were placed on the cupboards so that she could find the utensils she needed to use for cookery. While this pupil needed one-to-one support, specialised equipment and adapted learning materials, some pupils may only need monitoring and adapted learning materials, depending on the severity of the visual impairment.

The learning environment

Physical environment

- Risk assessment – ensure a risk assessment is carried out in order to cater for the individual pupil's needs.
- Use large print/Braille signs that are obvious, well placed and clearly noticeable.
- Highlight steps with yellow or white paint lines.

- Fit handrails to assist the visually impaired pupil with their mobility.
- Use tactile trails consisting of bumpy materials at hand height to assist the individual with going to different parts of the school including the toilets, dining hall, gym.
- Fit different floor coverings in different areas of the school to indicate a change of environment.

If your environment is not suitable and will need adaptations, use the following as a checklist to ensure the adaptations are made prior to the pupil arriving at the school:

- When will the work take place?
- Has a risk assessment been carried out to ensure there are no places which are unsafe for the child with visual impairment to be?
- Are the signs around the school at the correct height and clearly visible?

In the classroom

- Achieve the correct lighting level for the pupils, as some may be sensitive to light while others may need more light.
- Fit window blinds to reduce the glare from sunlight.
- Always stand against a wall when teaching rather than against the window as pupils will not be able to see you with the light behind you.
- Use black (not coloured) pen on the whiteboard.
- Ensure you are consistent with materials. Keep them in the same place at all times.

Social environment

- Any member of staff working with a pupil with visual impairment should be aware of the pupils' individuals needs.
- Always read out any material which is presented on the whiteboard.
- To offer an inclusive environment ensure sighted pupils are able to join in with games only normally available for visually impaired pupils.
- Do not isolate pupils with visual impairment at break times and lunch times, encourage independence.

Adapted from Salisbury (2008, p8–10)

Why not try this?

Identify a lesson you have already planned and need to prepare handouts for and follow this checklist:

1. Identify the title of the lesson.
2. Identify the aim of the lesson.
3. Identify the objectives of the lesson.
4. Identify what materials you will need in order to deliver the lesson.
5. Adapt these activities for a pupil with visual impairment.

Prior to planning the lesson think about the following:

● The child's interests.
● Which teaching methods work best with the child?
● How can you facilitate opportunities for developing the child's independence?
● How can you best facilitate the learning of the child?

Why not try this?

Answer the following questions to reinforce your learning about working with visually impaired pupils:

● What do you understand your role as their teacher to be?
● How can you use TA support effectively to assist a pupil with visual impairment?

TOP TIP!

When considering the educational needs of pupils with visual impairments, some general strategies apply as follows:

- Do not presume that the pupil needs assistance at all times – ask.

- Always talk directly to the pupil and call them by their name.

- Do not presume that because the pupil has visual impairment he/she is unable to complete any task set, it may be that the task just needs modifying to suit the needs of the individual.

- Always consider seating arrangements to ensure the pupil is able to use any existing vision.

- Ensure the lighting is appropriate for the individual pupil.

- Consider the physical layout of the classroom and familiarise the pupil with the layout.

- Allow extra time for completion of tasks.

- Use peer mentoring to assist students who may need help with moving from one classroom to another classroom.

- Train all staff who will be working with a pupil with a visual impairment.

- Encourage pupils with visual problems to become independent learners and create opportunities for these pupils to develop their independence.

Hints and tips for teachers

- Ascertain what the child's visual difficulties are.
- Offer the use of visual aids including magnifiers.
- Ensure the child is seated in an appropriate place in the classroom.
- Eliminate any glare from the sunlight, ensuring that lighting is appropriate.
- Plan lessons with the child's individual visual needs in mind.
- Use large-print handouts and books if and when appropriate.
- Use coloured paper (depending on the nature of the visual impairment) with the correct print size – enlarge the print size if necessary.
- When preparing tasks, make sure that instructions are clearly visible and are also made orally.
- Offer practical hands-on experience wherever possible during a task.

In addition to these tips there are various technology devices that may assist individuals with visual impairments. Here are some examples of the devices that may help develop the independence of pupils with visual impairments:

clock/watch with braille face

audible clock/watch

appliances clearly labelled with larger numbers (e.g. microwave)

talking thermometer

large-button telephone

voice output communication aid

laptop computer with voice output

writing with symbols (picture system)

Braille writer

talking scales.

Key ideas summary

- Think about what you have learnt about visual impairments.
- How might you identify whether a pupil has a visual impairment?
- What strategies can you put into place in the classroom to ensure that a pupil with visual impairment is able to be included effectively?
- How can you overcome any barriers to learning that a pupil with visual impairment may face?

Going further

References and further reading

Davis, P. (2003) *Including Children with Visual Impairment in Mainstream Schools: A Practical Guide*, London: David Fulton.

National Health Service (2009) *Visual Impairment*, http://www.nhs.uk/Conditions/Visual-impairment/Pages/Introduction.aspx, accessed July 2009.

Salisbury, R. (2008) *Teaching Pupils with Visual Impairment: A Guide to making the School Curriculum accessible*, Abingdon: Routledge.

Smith, T.E.C., Polloway, E.A., Patton, J.R. and Dowdy, C.A. (2008) (5th edn) *Teaching Students with Special Educational Needs in Inclusive Settings*, Harlow: Prentice Hall.

Glossary

ABC Antecedent, behaviour, consequence.

ADHD The American Psychiatric Association set out the criteria for attention deficit hyperactivity disorder which form the diagnosis of ADHD.

ASD Autistic Spectrum Disorder.

Blindness Refers to a person who has severe sight loss.

Cataracts A clouding which causes temporary blindness.

Central vision loss Prevents an individual from seeing fine detail.

Cognitive Relates to the mental processes of perceiving, thinking and remembering.

DDA Disability Discrimination Act 1995.

Dopamine A type of neurotransmitter present in regions of the brain that regulate movement, motivation and the feeling of pleasure.

Echolalia Refers to the automatic repetition of speech made by another person.

Functional vision A term which refers to what an individual is able to see.

Glaucoma A disease whereby the optic nerve is damaged which causes temporary blindness.

Hyperactivity A higher than normal level of activity; can be used to describe increased action of a body function including hormone production or behaviour.

May result in the person always fidgeting, moving, being unable to concentrate and talking too much.

Inattention A child's inability to pay or sustain attention.

Impulsiveness The trait of acting on impulse without reflection. An impulsive child may act without taking the consequences into consideration.

Inclusive Education A commitment to ensuring all children, regardless of disabilities, may be included in mainstream education.

Individual Education Plan (IEP) The IEP is a planning, teaching and reviewing tool. It is a working document for all teaching staff recording key short-term targets and strategies for an individual pupil that are different from or additional to those in place for the rest of the group or class.

Mascular degeneration This is a common cause of reduced vision, which is as a result of wear and tear on the eye.

Neurological Relates to the body's nervous system which oversees and controls all body functions.

Partial sightedness Refers to a person who is partially sighted.

Peripheral vision loss In contrast to Central vision loss, this may result in tunnel vision.

Poor acuity Refers to the clarity or sharpness of the overall image.

School Action When a class or subject teacher identify that a pupil has special educational needs they provide interventions that are additional to or different from those provided as part of the school's usual differentiated curriculum offer and strategies. An **IEP** will usually be devised.

School Action Plus When a class or subject teacher and the SENCO are provided with advice or support from outside specialists, so that alternative interventions of strategies to those provided for the pupil through School Action can be put in place. A new **IEP** will usually be devised.

SEBD Social, emotional and behavioural difficulties.

SEN special educational needs.

SENCO special educational needs coordinator.

SENDA Special Educational Needs and Disability Act 2001.

Index

Classroom Gems

Innovative resources, inspiring creativity across the school curriculum

Designed with busy teachers in mind, the Classroom Gems series draws together an extensive selection of practical, tried-and-tested, off-the-shelf ideas, games and activities, guaranteed to transform any lesson or classroom in an instant.

Games and activities for
Primary Modern Foreign Languages

© 2008 Paperback 336pp
ISBN: 9781405873925

Practical ideas, games and activities for the
Primary Classroom
Paul Barron

© 2008 Paperback 312pp
ISBN: 9781405859455

Games, ideas and activities for
Primary PE
Will Allen

© 2009 Paperback 224pp
ISBN: 9781408220382

Games, ideas and activities for
Learning Outside the Primary Classroom
Paul Barron

© 2009 Paperback 256pp
ISBN: 9781408225608

Games, ideas and activities for
Primary Mathematics
John Dabell

© 2009 Paperback 304pp
ISBN: 9781408223208

Games, ideas and activities for
Primary Humanities
Richard Green

© 2009 Paperback 304pp
ISBN: 9781408228098

Games, ideas and activities for
Primary Music
Donna Minto

© 2009 Paperback 304pp
ISBN: 9781408223260

Games, ideas and activities for
Primary Drama
Michael Theodorou

© 2009 Paperback 304pp
ISBN: 9781408223291

Games, ideas and activities for
Early Years Phonics
Lynn Cousins and Gill Coulson

© 2009 Paperback 304pp
ISBN: 9781408224359

Creative activities for the
Secondary Classroom
Mark Latraw

© 2009 Paperback 256pp
ISBN: 9781408225578

Games, ideas and activities for
Primary Science
John Dabell

© 2010 Paperback 304pp
ISBN: 9781408223239

Games, ideas and activities for
Primary Literacy
Hazel Glynne and Amanda Snowden

© 2010 Paperback 336pp
ISBN: 9781408225516

'Easily navigable, allowing teachers to choose the right activity quickly and easily, these invaluable resources are guaranteed to save time and are a must-have tool to plan, prepare and deliver first-rate lessons'

Longman
is an imprint of

PEARSON

The Essential Guides Series

Practical skills for teachers

The Essential Guides series offers a wealth of practical support, inspiration and guidance for NQTs and more experienced teachers ready to implement into their classroom. The books provide practical advice and tips on the core aspects of teaching and everyday classroom issues, such as planning, assessment, behaviour and ICT. The Essential Guides are invaluable resources that will help teachers to successfully navigate the challenges of the profession.

The Essential Guide to
Successful School Trips
John Trant

© 2010 paperback
ISBN 978-1-4082-0447-4

The Essential Guide to
Using ICT Creatively in the Primary Classroom
Steve Woods

© 2010 paperback
ISBN 978-1-4082-2497-7

The Essential Guide to
Secondary Teaching
Susan Davies

© 2010 paperback
ISBN 978-1-4082-2452-6

The Essential Guide to
Classroom Assessment
Paul Dix

© 2010 paperback
ISBN 978-1-4082-3025-1

The Essential Guide to
Taking Care of Behaviour
(second edition)
Paul Dix

© 2010 paperback
ISBN 978-1-4082-2554-7

The Essential Guide to
Shaping Children's Behaviour in the Early Years
Lynn Cousins

© 2010 paperback
ISBN 978-1-4082-2502-8

The Essential Guide to
Teaching 14-19 Diplomas
Lynn Senior

© 2010 paperback
ISBN 978-1-4082-2549-3

Longman
is an imprint of

PEARSON

Practical skills for teachers